Model Railway Constructor
ANNUAL 1986

£4.95

Model Railway Constructor

ANNUAL 1986

Edited by Chris Leigh

IA
LONDON
IAN ALLAN LTD

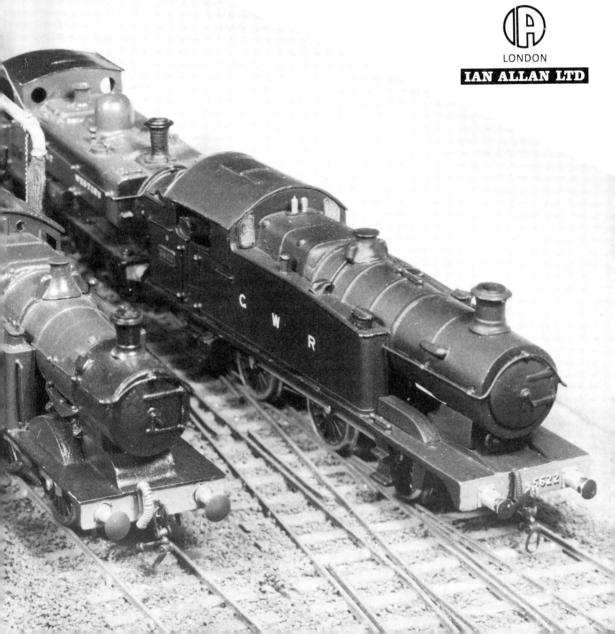

Contents

Previous page:
Sunday afternoon on Dowlais Cae Harris shed L to R front, Ex RR Class 5 No 611, Class M No 33, Class P No 83, GW 5622; rear Class S No 95 Ex TVR 41 No 599, GW 4268 and 5717. The doors still do not seem to have been repaired! The Cardiff 4mm Group layout was featured in *MRC* **March 1985.**
Brian Monaghan

First published 1985

ISBN 0 7110 1508 2

Published by Ian Allan Ltd, Shepperton, Surrey; and printed by Ian Allan Printing Ltd at their works at Coombelands in Runnymede, England.

Locomotives on shed at Brocknails on the 009 layout of Chester MRC, described in *MRC* **March 1984.**
Brian Monaghan

BR-Built Ventilated Fruit Vans

Paul W. Bartlett, Trevor Mann and David Monk-Steel

(British Railways Historical Study Group &
Historical Model Railway Society)

Because fresh fruit and vegetables are highly perishable, specially designed railway wagons have been used for their carriage for many years. These wagons have two important features in common: they have more ventilation than ordinary vans and for many years they have been equipped with continuous brakes so they could work in the fastest freight trains. Indeed many ventilated fruit vans were built to the standards of coaching stock, with through steam pipes and improved suspension, so that they could work in any passenger train and at passenger train speeds. This article will describe and illustrate the vehicles which BR built as wagons for fresh produce and not those in the non-passenger carrying coaching fleet. Although specialised, they do allow us to illustrate several vans which were similar to standard vans and also to illustrate the three common standard vacuum-brake underframes used during the early years of BR.

Sources of Traffic

The various 'Gardens of England' were the sources of fruit traffic, notably Kent, the Channel Islands, the far south-west, the Vale of Evesham, Humberside, lowland Scotland and the Fens of East Anglia. The different pre-Nationalisation companies coped with this traffic in varying ways, often using general-purpose well ventilated vehicles which could also be used for other traffic, including milk in churns and general postal traffic, the latter particularly at Christmas time.

Pre-Nationalisation

The Southern Railway did not brand any of its wagons for fruit traffic. It relied upon the large numbers of utility vans in the non-passenger carrying fleet; the bogie and 4-wheel CCTs, and the PMV. Each of these had side ventilators in addition to those in the ends.

The LMS built well ventilated 6-wheel non-passenger carrying vans for fruit, some of which were also branded for milk (see *An illustrated history of LMS coaches 1923-1957*, D. Jenkinson & R. J. Essery; Oxford Publishing Co). They also built six fruit vans in 1946 which were similar to their ordinary merchandise vans except that pocket ventilators were located in the sides and eight torpedo ventilators in the roof (see *An illustrated history of LMS wagons. Vol 1*, R. J. Essery; Oxford Publishing Co).

The Great Western had many vans suitable for fruit; the wagon diagram book allocated section Y to these and the Banana vans (see *GWR Wagons. Vol 2*, Atkins, Beard, Hyde, & Tourret; David & Charles). The means of ventilation varied. Paired bonnet ventilators in the ends were normal and sides often had ventilation slots between planks and/or panels of slotted ventilators. The GWR also had similar vehicles in the non-passenger carrying fleet. In addition their numerous 4-wheel and bogie Siphons, which were built to carry milk in churns, were also suitable for this traffic if required. The Siphons have been discussed in a series by J. Slinn in *Volumes 11* and *12* of the *Journal of the HMRS*.

In contrast to the other Companies, the non-passenger carrying coaching stock of the LNER was generally poorly ventilated and not suitable for fruit. However they had many freight stock Fruit vans which were 17ft 6in over headstocks. Although differing in construction, from the mid-1930s they tended to standardise on

1: No E277977, an LNER Fruit van built at Darlington in 1945. It had the simple pre-1964 lettering style, with the 'FRUIT' cast plate on the door, when photographed at Feltham in April 1968. The slatted end ventilators are obvious.
Paul W. Bartlett

an unusual means of ventilation, the lower half of the end of the vans being a series of slatted louvres (see *A pictorial record of LNER wagons*, P. Tatlow; Oxford Publishing Co, 1976).

BR-built Wagons

Thus when BR was formed it had a range of ideas about fruit van design from which to draw. As with other wagon types, BR continued to build a number of different designs and only later introduced a unified one. This tendency was even more noticeable with the non-passenger carrying vans, with GWR and SR designs being built until about 1957.

The BR-built vans described in detail here had similarities. The underframes were all 17ft 6in over headstocks with a wheelbase of 10ft and continuous vacuum brake. All were painted either freight stock red or bauxite (although BR always called it red, the pigment which provided the red was changed from a poor quality bauxite which was used in the early years of BR and gave a distinctly orange hue to the

finish, to bauxite of Larne quality as had been used by the LMS and gave a browner bauxite finish). Details of the lettering are given in the article where appropriate, and all lettering was in white paint.

LNER Design

The first to be considered were those based on LNER practice. This design was already numerous as 1,500 had been built post-war to LNER orders. These had been given diagram number 187 and BR continued to build them by ordering a single batch of 750, the largest single order for Fruit vans placed by BR. They were given diagram number 1/232 by BR. The Table shows the unusual feature about this batch – they were numbered into the B75 series which was reserved for ordinary vans. Either the order was placed before this was decided or it was intended to build a batch of ordinary LNER vans which were altered to be Fruit vans before production began. In fact, BR built no ordinary vans of LNER design, whereas they did build some of each of the other Companies.

Building and Numbering Details of BR-built Fruit Vans:

Diag No.	Lot No.	Qnty	Builder	Year	Running numbers	Underframe	Body type
1/230	2018	200	Wolverton	1949/50	B875000-875199	LMS clasp	LMS plyside, corrugated end
1/230	2135	250	Darlington	1950-2	B875300-875549	LNER clasp	LMS plyside, corrugated end
1/231	2084	100	Swindon	1949	B875200-875299	RCH vacuum	GWR plyside, ply end
1/232	2134	750	Darlington	1950	B754430-755179	LNER clasp	LNER plyside, ply end
1/233	2472	100	Darlington	1953	B875550-875649	RCH vacuum	BR plyside, corrugated end
1/233	2738	100	Darlington	1955	B875650-875749	RCH vacuum	BR plyside, corrugated end
1/233	3009	100	Darlington	1957	B875750-875849	RCH vacuum	BR plyside, corrugated end
1/234	3392	6	Wolverton	1962	B784285-784290	BR/LMS clasp	BR plyside, corrugated end

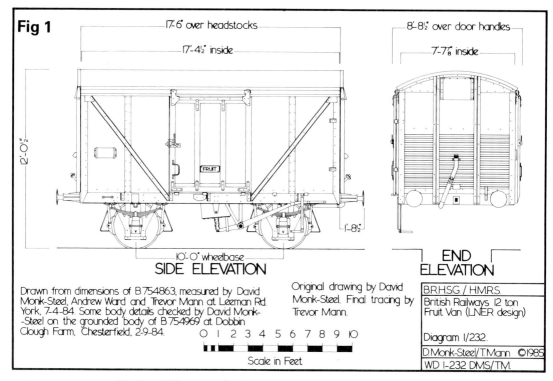

Fig 1

17'-6" over headstocks

17'-4½" inside

8'-8½" over door handles

7'-7⅞" inside

12'-0½"

1'-8½"

SIDE ELEVATION

END ELEVATION

10'-0" wheelbase

Drawn from dimensions of B754863, measured by David Monk-Steel, Andrew Ward and Trevor Mann at Leeman Rd. York, 7-4-84. Some body details checked by David Monk-Steel on the grounded body of B754969 at Dobbin Clough Farm, Chesterfield, 2-9-84.

Original drawing by David Monk-Steel. Final tracing by Trevor Mann.

B.R.HSG / H.M.R.S.
British Railways 12 ton Fruit Van (LNER design)

Diagram 1/232.

D.Monk-Steel/T.Mann ©1985

WD 1-232 DMS/TM.

0 1 2 3 4 5 6 7 8 9 10

Scale in Feet

As can be seen in **Fig 1** and **Photographs 1 and 2** the Fruit vans were very similar to the standard van, and had the characteristic LNER clasp vacuum-brake which had two V-hangers on one side and only one on the other, the side with the vacuum cylinder. Standard fittings were upright vacuum pipes, full web buffers and screw link couplings. The body was constructed entirely of plywood with a sliding door. The diagonal strapping on the side was U-channel and the door had two vertical flat strappings. No B754952 also had a horizontal strip across the door. There were no ventilators in the side of the body. The ends had both a single conventional bonnet ventilator and also a series of slatted ventilators in the lower part. In addition the roof had three pairs of torpedo ventilators. These may not be shown by our Fig 1 because they were often removed when the wagons were repaired during later years.

One unusual feature of these vans was the fixing of a cast plate to the door which bore the simple 'FRUIT' legend. Many of these wagons were branded 'Return empty to Whitemoor GE'. This was on the left-hand side above the number. When the corporate image style of lettering was introduced, with the number and data in a panel, they had the 'FRUIT' brand as the top line with the 'Return to . . .' above, also in separate box.

2: No B754976, a BR-built LNER-design Fruit van which, as well as having the cast 'FRUIT' plate picked out in white, has the branding 'FRUIT ONLY, RETURN EMPTY TO WHITEMOOR G.E.' above the number. Photographed at Staines in April 1968. *Paul W. Bartlett*

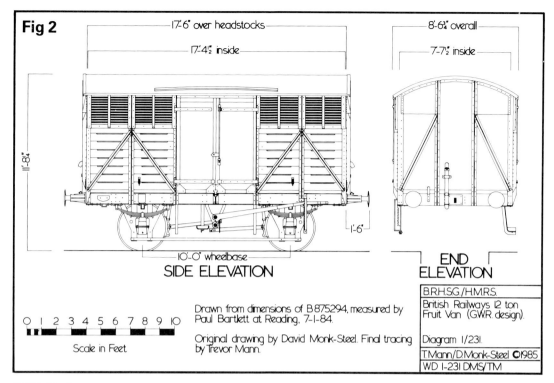

Fig 2

17′-6″ over headstocks

17′-4½″ inside

8′-6¼″ overall

7′-7½″ inside

11′-8¼″

1′-6″

10′-0″ wheelbase

SIDE ELEVATION

END ELEVATION

0 1 2 3 4 5 6 7 8 9 10

Scale in Feet

Drawn from dimensions of B.875294, measured by Paul Bartlett at Reading, 7-1-84.

Original drawing by David Monk-Steel. Final tracing by Trevor Mann.

B.R.H.S.G./H.M.R.S.

British Railways 12 ton Fruit Van (GWR. design).

Diagram 1/231.

T.Mann/D.Monk-Steel ©1985

WD 1-231 DMS/TM

GWR Design

The GWR design of fruit van was quite different. Based on the GWR diagram Y8 of which 200 were built in 1937-8, they were initially given GW/BR diagram number Y13 which became BR diagram 1/231. As can be seen in **Fig 2** and **Photograph 3** it had the standard RCH vacuum-brake underframe with a drop-down vacuum pipe, GWR style 'instanter' couplings and full web buffers. Offset to the left of the centre line was a step. Why this was provided is not clear, perhaps, because much of the trade was seasonal and from small yards, loading facilities such as banks were unavailable and staff had to be able to climb into the wagons to load them from the ground.

The body was similar to the ordinary GWR van, but that had been of planked construction. The end was made of plywood and had two bonnet ventilators. It would appear that no ventilators were put in the roof. The sides had a pair of plywood cupboard doors. The remainder of the side was ventilated and each panel either side of the doors was split into two. The upper part of the side was a series of slats and the lower part of the side was planked. The top edge of each plank was neatly chamfered to allow for some further ventilation. There were two diagonal T-angle strappings on each side, which gave an unusual appearance.

The lettering was on the inside of the triangle formed by the strapping at either end, with the 'FRUIT' branding on the third or fourth plank. During the early 1960s the upper slats were removed from some vans and replaced by plywood sheets, an example of this being No B875283. This wagon also had the boxed-in lettering style with the brand 'VANFIT'. The wagon measured for **Fig 2** still had Return to Honeybourne (WR) on the inside, so it was used for traffic from the Vale of Evesham in Worcestershire.

3: Appears on page 45.

4: No DB875120, a BR Fruit van of LMS design, built at Wolverton in 1950. This van, which was plated to work with ballast cleaner No DB965023, when photographed at Lowestoft in August 1980, has the 'VENTILATED FRUIT VAN' centrally on the door, an unusual position. It has a two-part end and LMS clasp brake underframe.
Paul W. Bartlett

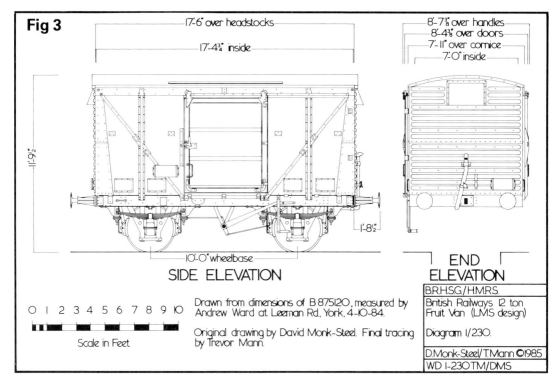

Fig 3

17'-6" over headstocks

17'-4¾" inside

11'-9½"

8'-7⅜" over handles
8'-4⅜" over doors
7'-11" over cornice
7'-0" inside

1'-8½"

10'-0" wheelbase

SIDE ELEVATION

END ELEVATION

0 1 2 3 4 5 6 7 8 9 10	Drawn from dimensions of B 875120, measured by Andrew Ward at Leeman Rd., York, 4-10-84.	B.R.H.S.G./H.M.R.S.
Scale in Feet	Original drawing by David Monk-Steel. Final tracing by Trevor Mann.	British Railways 12 ton Fruit Van (LMS design)
		Diagram 1/230.
		D.Monk-Steel/T.Mann ©1985
		WD 1-230 TM/DMS

LMS Design

After World War 2 the LMS introduced a third approach to increasing ventilation, although they built only six vans of diagram 2112 as an experiment. BR quickly introduced 450 similar wagons which received diagram 1/230. This is illustrated by **Fig 3** and **Photographs 4 and 5**. Like the LMS wagons they had four pocket ventilators

5: KDB875410 a BR Fruit van of LMS design which, because it was built at Darlington in 1950, has LNER clasp brake. It was photographed at Reading in July 1977 when it was being used by the Signal works there. The boxed in style of lettering with 'FRUIT' on the top line can be seen.
Paul W. Bartlett

6: A close-up of the pocket ventilator of No DB875120. Notice the maintenance record panel above it.
Paul W. Bartlett

7: Appears on page 45.

8: No B784288, a Ventilated 'Vanwide' with the TOPS code VWV seen at Horwich Works in August 1980. The shutters are covering the side ventilator, and the plating over of the hole for the end ventilator is noticeable. It has the LMS-style underframe without J-hanger spring hangers and large 'VENTILATED VAN' lettering which it has carried from when it was new in 1962. The number is in a post-1964 box which is incorrectly drawn as broken lines. *Paul W. Bartlett*

(see **Photograph 6**) low down on the plywood sides, and a sliding door. Each panel on either side was supported by a U-channel vertical stanchion and also a flat diagonal. Also on the side were four plates in a row each of which had three bolts. These held shelves which folded up inside the van. The door had two horizontal strips to reinforce it. These arrangements made the appearance distinctive from the LNER van.

Each end had a single bonnet ventilator but, unlike the LMS-built wagons which had plywood ends, all the BR-built wagons had corrugated metal ends. There were at least two variants of these ends; most of lot 2018 had an end which was made of two parts, these overlapped above the eighth corrugation above the headstock. The remainder of lot 2018 and possibly all of lot 2135 had an end made from three pieces of steel; they had an additional overlap immediately below the end ventilator. All of these joints had a row of bolts where the steel overlapped. Another difference from the LMS-built wagons was in the roof ventilators – they had had eight torpedo ventilators but none were fitted to the BR-built wagons. This is surprising as the contemporary ordinary vans, of similar design, were built with four ventilators.

The underframe designs introduce a complication to this diagram. Lot 2018, being built at the ex-LMS works at Wolverton, was given the standard LMS arrangement of clasp brake (see **Photograph 4**). They had upright vacuum pipe, screw couplings, full web buffers and two piece axleboxes. A central V-hanger, a short brake lever and rubber auxiliary spring hangers (J-hangers) were fitted. The other lot, No 2135, was built at the ex-LNER Darlington (Faverdale) works so received the standard LNER clasp brake arrangement (see **Photograph 5**), as described and illustrated for the LNER Fruit van earlier. They had drop-down vacuum pipes, screw link couplings and full web buffers.

The pocket ventilators on the side made for some difficulty in positioning the lettering. Early on, this was further complicated by a cast plate with 'RETURN EMPTY TO EVESHAM LMR' being positioned immediately above the left-hand ventilator. Together they meant that the number, which should have been in the lower left-hand corner, was moved high up, with the '12t' and 'VENTILATED FRUIT VAN' higher still. These cast plates were subsequently removed but this long code name remained common until the boxed-in style of lettering was introduced. By then patch repairs on this panel sometimes meant that the data panel could be very high up, or the 'FRUIT' or 'FRUIT VAN' branding had to be separated from the number. Sometimes it was placed on one or other of the left-hand ventilators. Usually care was taken not to overlap lettering onto the section where the steel of the end wrapped around the side. On the right-hand side it was common to place the 'XP', tare and 'wb10-0' on the steel overlap or above the ventilator. In later years the maintenance panel was placed here with the other markings higher up. It was not usual to have 'Return to . . .' brandings on these vans, although they commonly worked to Whitemoor for Fenland fruit and vegetables, as well as to Evesham.

BR Design

In 1953 BR introduced a design of Fruit van based upon the contemporary standard van. This was given diagram 1/233 and is illustrated by **Fig 4** and **Photograph 7**. Between 1953 and 1957 three batches were built, all of which were similar in appearance. They followed the LMS practice by using pocket ventilators low down on the body side and by having the same metal plates which show the position of the internal folding shelves. The body was similar to the GWR van design and made of plywood. The ends were of conventional corrugated construction with a single bonnet ventilator. Some, possibly all, of lot 2472 had the three-part end as used on lot 2135. The later lots had a two-part end like many of lot 2018. No roof ventilators were fitted.

The underframes were all of the same RCH vacuum-brake type with a single brake shoe on each wheel. They had drop-down vacuum pipe, screw couplings and full web buffers. Two-piece axleboxes were common. The livery was similar to the LMS-design wagons, with the same problems of positioning the lettering caused by the pocket ventilators. Like them they were often branded with the full 'VENTILATED FRUIT VAN'.

9: No 21 83 238 2 622-0, an Italian ferry van which is suitable for fresh produce as it has ventilators low down in the end, and both high and low on the side. The van was built in about 1970 and is typical of modern European vans. It was photographed at Mossend in July 1984. *Paul W. Bartlett*

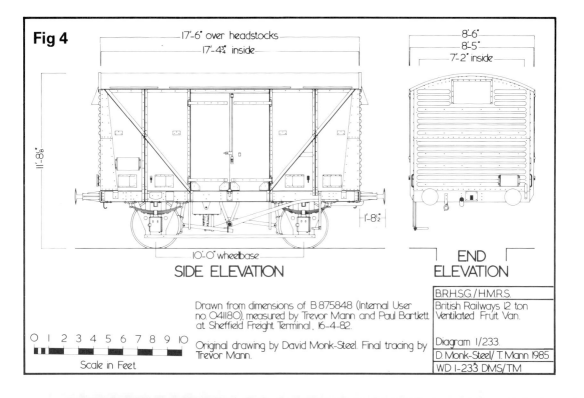

Fig 4

17'-6" over headstocks
17'-4¾" inside

8'-6"
8'-5"
7'-2" inside

11'-8⅝"

1'-8½"

10'-0" wheelbase

SIDE ELEVATION

END ELEVATION

Drawn from dimensions of B.875848 (Internal User no. 041180), measured by Trevor Mann and Paul Bartlett at Sheffield Freight Terminal, 16-4-82.

Original drawing by David Monk-Steel. Final tracing by Trevor Mann.

0 1 2 3 4 5 6 7 8 9 10
Scale in Feet

| B.R.H.S.G./H.M.R.S. |
| British Railways 12 ton Ventilated Fruit Van. |
| Diagram 1/233. |
| D. Monk-Steel/ T. Mann 1985 |
| WD 1-233 DMS/TM |

Ventilated 'Vanwide'

One design remains to be discussed in detail. BR experimented with several ways of coping with the introduction of pallet loading of goods. The most successful early design was the 'Vanwide'. Between 1961 and 1963 2,000 were built to three lots. As part of lot 3392, six 'Vanwides' were built with additional ventilation in the doors. These were given diagram 1/234 (see **Photograph 8**). The sides were made of plywood and had a pair of sliding doors which gave a 9ft door opening. There was a large ventilator high up in each of these doors which were similar to European practice, with a shutter which could be raised from below. The two-part corrugated end was of conventional construction but, rather surprisingly, the hole for the bonnet ventilator was plated over. There were no roof ventilators.

The underframe, like those of all the 'Vanwides', was unusual. BR returned to using the LMS style of clasp brake (none of the Fruit vans used the standard BR clasp brake underframe). Unlike the LMS wagons no auxiliary rubber spring hangers were fitted, although they did have the short brake lever and central V-hanger of this design. They had Dowty hydraulic buffers, 'instanter' couplings, drop-down vacuum pipe and one-piece axleboxes.

The lettering was rather unusual. The 'XP', 'wb10-0' and tare were on the extreme right-hand end. The number and '12T' was on the left-hand door and 'VENTILATED VAN' was in unusually large letters on the right-hand door with 'EMPTY TO MARAZION W.R.' below. The latter was removed by the mid-1960s but indicates that the vans were used for carrying flowers and vegetables from the Scilly Islands, which are particularly noted for their early Narcissi. They may also have carried Cornish early potatoes.

Use and Condemnation

The 10ft wheelbase Fruit vans were frequently used like ordinary vans. Condemnation began in the early 1970s and, except for the 'Vanwide' type, the last were withdrawn at the end of 1976 which, for those based on the BR standard van, was six years earlier than their contemporaries. The ventilated 'Vanwides' had been used as ordinary 'Vanwides' for many years and like them were withdrawn at the end of 1983. At that time many of the ordinary 'Vanwides' were converted to airbrake for MOD traffic, but these ventilated vans were not included.

A few Fruit vans remain in Engineers use, sometimes working as tool vans with ballast cleaners. Interestingly the Research division at Derby retained a rake of the BR design until 1982 as a test train.

It would be wrong if we left the impression that this is the end of the story of fresh fruit and vegetables being carried on BR. Although very little is carried internally, cross-Channel traffic is important. At much the same time as the ventilated 'Vanwide' was introduced, BR began building the much larger Ferry vans. Full details of these were given in our article in *Model Railway Constructor Annual 1985* pp18-29. These had four large ventilators in each side which could be covered by shutters in the same way as those of the Ventilated 'Vanwide'. Like the contemporary European ferry vans (see **Photograph 9**) they could be used for fresh produce and can be considered as a modern Fruit van.

In more recent years simple ventilation has become less suitable for keeping fresh produce in condition, especially as supermarkets have demanded cold chain transport. To cope with this the large European private operators, Interfrigo of Italy and Transfesa of Spain, have insulated vans which have ice boxes in either end. Vans of this type have existed for many years but both fleets have grown in recent years. This cool chain transport is adequate for the few days it takes the fast freight trains to travel from southern Europe to Britain.

Modelling Possibilities

We hope that this article has suitably introduced these interesting wagons. As they could be worked either in block trains or individually, they could be used on any layout. During the 1950s and 1960s they could be seen at any local yard and, as the traffic they carried was seasonal, even the smallest model goods yard in an agricultural area could have large numbers of them, with all the accompanying organised chaos of road vehicles and hand loading.

Of the 10ft wheelbase vans Mainline make a nice model of the body of the distinctive GWR Fruit van, however it has planked ends and doors, so it represents one of the 1937-8 batch. Parkside make a kit of the LNER-style Fruit van. Unfortunately they only provide an RCH-type underframe which is unsuitable for either the LNER or BR-built versions. ABS Models make castings suitable for this alteration. Many years ago Tri-ang introduced a model of the ventilated 'Vanwide'. This is still available from Hornby but, like many of their models, it is too short and has other proportional errors.

Suitable plywood-bodied models of the BR and LMS ordinary vans are not available. If they were, the Fruit vans would be simple conversions from them. As well as adding representations of the pocket ventilators, a few small bolts would indicate the position of the internal folding shelves. It is possible to alter the Hornby Banana van into the BR plywood van by adding the end ventilators and removing some of the strapping from the door and either side of it. With some suitable lettering this would be a simple way to introduce some distinctive models to any layout. If a plywood LMS van does become available then the LMS van built on an LNER underframe may even catch out some of your supposedly knowledgeable friends. Alternatively these are quite simple vans, which lend themselves to scratch building. If necessary the corrugated ends could be borrowed from other kits.

10: KDB875294, a BR-built GWR-design Fruit van which was in engineers use when seen at Shildon in April 1980. There is some rubber hosing and electric cable running up the diagonal stanchion at the near end. The FRUIT branding is on the fourth plank. The plain plywood end shows, with a patch repair. *Paul W. Bartlett*

Longbridge in the 1960s – A prototype worth modelling

It is not generally realised that the Austin Motor Company's Longbridge plant, now part of British Leyland, contained a major industrial railway system. The factory stands alongside the Birmingham-Bromsgrove main line and there is now actually a Longbridge station on the main line, forming the southern limit of West Midlands PTE's cross city link suburban service. Just north of the present station lies Halesowen Junction where the former Midland Railway branch line through Rubery to Halesowen diverged. At Halesowen the branch formed an end-on junction with the GWR branch from Old Hill, thus providing a through route.

When I came to know Longbridge, the only station was a private one, used only by workmen's trains and situated in the heart of the Austin works. The station and the branch line were, in fact, BR owned and operated but their situation was such that only Austin employees could gain access, and accordingly I counted myself lucky, one day in 1966, to be given a conducted tour of the Austin railway system.

The map shows how the system was laid out to serve factory buildings on both sides of the branch. To model it completely would require vast space, but one could easily take a third of the system – the area east of the A38 bridge, the station area, or the western yard area, and each would make an interesting layout in its own right. Selective compression to reduce the size would benefit the model by cramming the detail closer together.

Below:
'74XX' 0-6-0PT No 7429 heads the 18.09 workmen's train to Old Hill, standing in the loop platform at Longbridge. The west works building forms the background. The station lamps are pure Midland Railway, but otherwise there are only basic corrugated platform shelters. The date, 10 April 1958. *E. J. Dew*

At the time of my visit, Austin owned five locomotives, one of which was out of use as BR had banned it from using their track pending wheel re-profiling. On the day of my visit the 0-6-0STs, *Austin 1*, *Victor* and *Vulcan* were in steam. The latter were two outside valve gear Bagnalls of 1952 vintage, acquired from the Steel Company of Wales. All three locomotives are now preserved.

The traffic within the works area provided much more variety than one might imagine. Workmen's trains had ceased to operate by the time of my visit, since they operated from the Halesowen direction and the branch had been severed by the demolition of Dowery Dell viaduct when it became unsafe. The trains had been formed of ex-GWR suburban stock, usually headed by '74XX' class pannier tanks, which were one of few types light enough to be permitted over the route.

After this, BR locomotives continued to work into the factory area with freight from the 'Midland' end, and during my visit a Class 25 diesel arrived to collect bogie 'Carflat' wagons loaded with new Minis and Riley Elfs. These cars were loaded from the station platforms which by then had had all structures except the footbridge removed.

In addition there were deliveries of sand and metal ingots to the foundry and supplies of fuel oil coming in, while 16ton mineral wagons loaded with swarf and metal scrap were sent out. There was quite a considerable fleet of internal-use private owner wagons, many of them antique open wagons,

used for movement of stores within the factory area and to make trips to the refuse destructor.

The track layout was thus complex, with rail access to almost every part of the factory. In some areas, particularly at the eastern end of the plant, there were some sharp gradients and tight curves. The centre of operations was the fine Midland Railway signal cabin, Longbridge East, situated close to the A38 road bridge which slices through the centre of the factory.

To the west of the bridge lay the station, with its main buildings standing actually on the bridge. The platforms were ash-surfaced and very grassy, comprising a single platform to the south of the branch 'main' line, and an island platform between this single track and the loop. By the time of my visit, this 'loop' was being used as the Austin 'main line' through the station. Beyond the station the branch petered out, and the works area ended in a large yard with numerous loop sidings, while another line headed north to the refuse destructor and the northwest factory area.

Below left:
Looking west from Longbridge with the branch to Halesowen completely overgrown, and the starter signal on the left. In the centre is the large yard area, with vans, open wagons and loaded carflats in evidence.

Below:
One of the loading bay areas for the west factory area with the shed marked No 1 on the map, visible in the centre. This area was adjacent to the western end of the station platform.

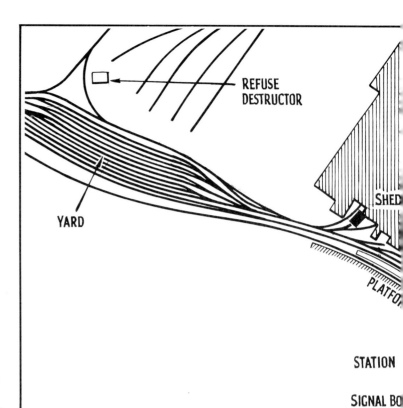

REFUSE
DESTRUCTOR

YARD

SHED

PLATFO

STATION

SIGNAL BO

Below:
Longbridge station, with empty
carflats standing on the former
branch line and new cars on the
platform awaiting loading. Signals
were operated from Longbridge
East signalbox to control
movements of Austin and BR trains.

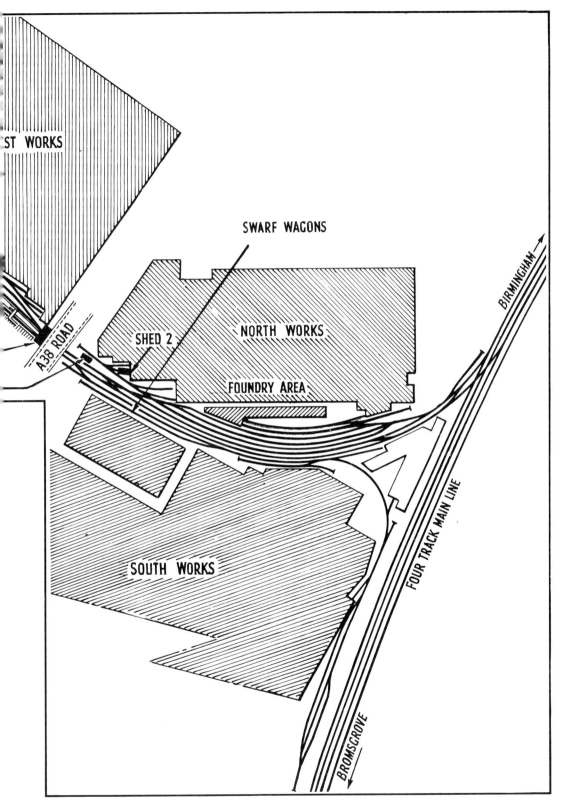

ST WORKS

SWARF WAGONS

A38 ROAD

SHED 2

NORTH WORKS

FOUNDRY AREA

BIRMINGHAM

FOUR TRACK MAIN LINE

SOUTH WORKS

BROMSGROVE

Above:
The west works seen from the station platform with car loading ramps in the foreground.

Right:
BR/Sulzer Type 2 No D5191 passes under the road bridge, bound for the west yard to collect carflats.

Below:
The road bridge with the station building just visible on top and the platforms visible through the arch. Centre is Longbridge East signalbox, a standard Midland Railway timber structure.

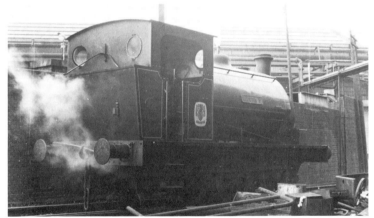

Above:
One of several internal user vehicles, a wooden-framed three-plank open wagon. It was painted mid grey with white lettering. This was near the locomotive workshops in the south works.

Left:
0-6-0ST *Austin 3* in lined green livery.

Below left:
Looking east with the foundry on the left, and *Austin 3* making a rousing start on slippery rails with a train of sand wagons.

Above left:
Bagnall 0-6-0ST *Victor* reversing towards the south works. Note the deep buffer beam to fend off obstructions and keep the locomotive upright if derailed.

Left:
The south works looking towards the junction. Swarf wagons on right include three Austin private owners among the standard 16ton minerals.

Below far left:
The north works and foundry seen from a locomotive descending the incline from the south works. In the centre are the 'main' lines through the works.

Below left:
The 0-6-0ST *Austin 1* inside the shed adjacent in the north works. Note the coaling stage on the left.

Top:
Austin 3 runs back past the foundry to collect empty sand wagons.

Above right:
A timber framed 7-plank wagon, No 138, branded for internal use only.

Right:
Bogie carflat wagons await loading at Longbridge station. A view looking from the station towards the south works, with an office building on the bridge over the station.

The Dumbiedykes Branch

D. Ford
An 00 Gauge Layout in the Loft

Unlike many model railway projects, Dumbiedykes was planned as a freelance branch line from the outset. It was to be based on British Railways circa 1966-68, located in no particular area, and the choice of stock and motive power entirely to the builder's whim. This way, you can run all your favourite locomotives, irrespective of origin, on one system!

The operation of the layout was to be prototypical, and based on single line branch practice. The area available was 22ft by 8ft which gave ample space for planning a layout with plenty of potential. It was decided that trains should run from a fiddle yard to a main branch terminus, and then to out-stations as additional services. Two out-stations were constructed and this gave an operational sequence as follows:

1. All trains from Kettledrummle Junction to Dumbiedykes.

2. From Dumbiedykes, trains can be returned to Kettledrummle or to either of the out-stations. From the out-stations, trains can only return to Dumbiedykes and then back to Kettledrummle.

Classes of trains run are as follows:

Class A: Through coaches from Kettledrummle to Dumbiedykes and return only.
Class B: Local passenger. To and from all stations on layout.
Class C: Parcels. To and from all stations on layout.
Class K: Local goods (general). From Kettledrummle to Dumbiedykes goods and cattle points.

Below:
The approach to Dumbiedykes showing the locomotive shed and goods yard. The Class 47 *Mammoth* waits outside the station as the DMU arrives from Balmawhapple. The shed is host to Type 2s Nos D6110 and D7596.

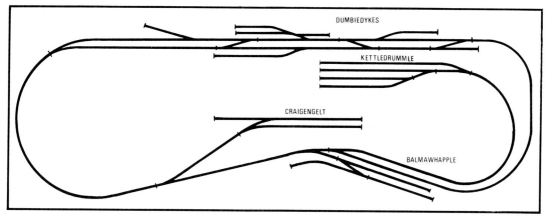

Class K: Fuel Wagons. To all points of layout where re-fuelling stages are constructed.

All trackwork is Peco Streamline, ballasted with bird grit and set directly on ½in chipboard. All points have motors mounted underneath and are controlled by the electric pencil method, with each station having its own control panel. Most sections are isolated by the points, and additional sections are controlled by on/off switches at the appropriate control panels.

Any train approaching the heel end of a point set against it, is electrically protected, and will stop automatically before a derailment can take place. Minimum point and curve radius is 3ft.

Scenery is constructed from polystyrene blocks, hammered to shape, covered with Mod-Roc, and finished off by hand with Polyfilla. Rockwork is painted to represent sandstone. Flock is applied to the upper surfaces with paint and glue, and trees are made from Lichen. Buildings and stations are a selection of kits and handbuilt items.

All motive power is proprietary, and detailed where necessary. To date, there are twelve locomotives and two fixed units in operation as follows:

D1670 *Mammoth*	Used on Class
D1011 *Western Thunderer*	A through
D1014 *Western Leviathan*	coaches
D6110 North British Type 2	

Below:
The autotrain stands in the bay at Dumbiedykes as *Western Leviathan* arrives on a through train. The prairie tank is shunting cattle wagons.

D7068 'Hymek' Type 3
D7596 BR Type 2
D5531 Brush Type 2
D6506 BRCW Type 3
D4106 EE Shunter
2213　Collett 0-6-0
44454 Fowler '4F' 0-6-0
6119　GWR large Prairie
–　　　Metro-Cammell 3-Car DMU
1412　Collett auto tank

All stock is kept in set formations for the various trains operated, and is a mixture of Lima, Mainline and Hornby plus the Airfix '14XX' tank and auto trailer.

Although the layout has a continuous run, the hidden section is not used for normal operation, as the layout normally employs end-to-end running, but if a locomotive requires running in, or 'Playing Trains' is required, then the hidden section is very useful. The station names were taken from old Scottish locomotives of Classes D11 and D30.

Many thanks are given to Martin Straker for his painstaking efforts to secure the photographs in the rather cramped loft area where the Dumbiedykes branch resides.

Below:
'Western' and Brush Type 4 diesels outside Dumbiedykes signalbox.

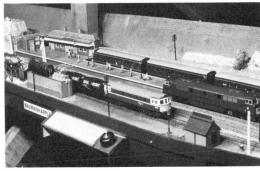

Above:
A busy scene at Balmawhapple with a DMU waiting in the bay, and Class 33 No D6506 on a tank train.

Above:
Two 'Westerns' run light to Dumbiedykes shed.

Scenic suggestions: 1

The Legend of the *Lucy Fisher*

Chris Leigh

Just as garden design benefits greatly from the inclusion of a pond or fountain or some use of water, so does layout design. There can be few layouts with a strong scenic element which does not include a stream, pond or river either as a major feature or as a filler for some awkward corner. Indeed, canals and the associated locks and narrow boats are almost too common a feature of model railway layouts these days. Of course, they have one major advantage in taking up only modest space, but if you have room for a small section of river or lake here is a suggestion for a vessel which is a star attraction in its own right.

While Queen Victoria ruled the mighty British Empire, an orphan boy was growing up deep in the jungle of West Africa. Kala, a she-ape of the tribe of Kerchak of the Great Apes raised the baby Tarzan as one of her own. As he grew he learned the laws of the wild and developed the strength, skills and courage of the animals. The advantage of human intelligence won him his place as King of the Jungle.

His simple existence was doomed, and one day his world was invaded by white men bringing a strange and alien civilisation. They travelled the jungle rivers on the paddle steamer *Lucy Fisher.* Tarzan came to know that in this other world he was John Clayton, the seventh Earl, Lord Greystoke.

This is the background to the many Tarzan films, the most recent of them, the Warner Brothers epic 'Greystoke – The Legend of Tarzan' being made in 1982. For this production a replica African paddle steamer of the Victorian era was constructed in England and shipped to Africa for the location sequences. After filming the vessel was returned to the UK and in 1984 it commenced operation from French Brothers' Old Windsor boathouse giving 35-minute cruises across historic Runnymede.

Thus, the *Lucy Fisher* is a near perfect subject for a modelling exercise. It has a delightful antiquated appearance and yet is quite relevant to a modern image layout. Indeed, the prototype operates within earshot of Class 455 EMUs rattling along the branch to Windsor. It is also a fairly straightforward vessel to model since the hull is flat-bottomed and very angular in shape. The most difficult items seemed likely to be the paddle wheel and the iron railings and stanchions supporting the awning.

It could almost be the heart of some tropical jungle, but it is in fact a quiet moment on the Thames in rural Surrey as the *Lucy Fisher* **rolls gently downstream. Note the bell under the eaves of the wheelhouse.**

First, though, a word of warning to the purists. The *Lucy Fisher* is a fraud. Despite her convincing appearance evident in the accompanying photographs, she is not quite what she seems, and the lack of smoke gives a clue. In fact, the vessel is diesel-engined and driven by a concealed screw. Don't be put off. Seen from the river bank she is almost silent, and as a passenger the throb of the engine is only a slight distraction and the thump of the churning paddles *feels* genuine enough.

Before starting the project I took a number of illustrations, both in black and white and in colour. I particularly wished to avoid views crowded with tourists, and views taken at the moorings were impractical because of obstructions, so it entailed watching for evening trips when there were few passengers. A few days of keeping an eye on the moorings while on my way home from work did the trick and I was able to get an unobstructed broadside view. I calculated the height of the wheelhouse and from this, with a lot of juggling with the enlarger, I made a photographic enlargement to 4mm scale. This gave an overall length around 62ft which I deemed accurate enough for my purposes without the bother of having to get permission to measure the vessel.

The overall width of 12ft was arrived at by careful calculation from photographs, my main concern being to get the proportions about right, rather than strict dimensional accuracy. The deck is flat, so from my length and width calculations I was able to draw a plan view onto ¼in thick balsa. Two thicknesses of this material glued together with Evo-Stik impact provide the hull. This was cut out,

carved and sanded to shape. A small surform proved useful in obtaining the very slight outwards rake of the hull sides. The stern was cut across absolutely square and vertical.

To obtain the correct bow profile and to give a smooth finish, the hull sides were overlaid with 20thou styrene sheet cut to the appropriate shape. This was also fixed with Evo-Stik which softens it just sufficiently to conform to the hull shape. Where the styrene sections join at the bow they were given a quick brush with solvent adhesive to weld the joint, which was then filed smooth. The deck was similarly surfaced with 30thou styrene. Before fitting in place, this was scribed with planking and the positions of the deckhouses and the boiler were marked. The boiler stands in a recess in the deck, so a square apperture was cut in the styrene before fixing. Within the aperture, the balsa hull was cut away to a depth of 3mm with the aid of craft knife and X-Acto fitted with a chisel blade.

The deck houses were built up from styrene sheet as straightforward boxes assembled with solvent adhesive and secured in place on the styrene deck. The leading one houses the engine and has a raised, curved section at the front over the access door. The side panels are louvred and one side has a cut-out to accommodate the wheelhouse ladder. I cut out the side panels and fitted overlapping strips of 20thou styrene to form the louvres. The rear deck house is similarly formed, but is full height and helps to support the awning.

To form the boiler, I cut a section of appropriate length from a piece of close-grained hardwood dowel. In the bottom of this, the centre was marked

The model showing the way in which it was slightly simplified with a flatter deck and the omission of the seats and Carley floats.

and drilled, and a No 6 wood screw was screwed in firmly but leaving about 1in of the screw still showing. With the screw head cut off, this portion was then set in the chuck of the electric drill. Using various files, and finishing with glass paper, I turned the dowel to the required dome shape. External ribbing and firebox doors were added from 10thou styrene before fixing the boiler in place in the deck recess.

While the drill was out, I also turned up the chimney using a piece of brass rod for the straight section, to which I had soldered the top ¾in of a large brass wood screw. The head of the screw provided just enough material for the flared chimney top. The chimney has to fit through the awning so it could not be fitted at this stage but it proved useful for locating the awning roof later on.

The main structure of the vessel consists of a steel framework comprising the upright supports for the awning, and all the deck railings. These are nothing like as complicated as they appear, and I built them up as two side units, adding the front and

Left:
The broadside view on which the author's model was largely based. The ladder to the wheelhouse can be seen beneath the left-hand life belt and the engineroom vents are immediately aft of the upper deck railing.

Right:
Detail of the paddle wheels showing the lightweight construction. The builder's plate on this side has gone missing.

rear rails as separate pieces once the model was nearly complete.

Using the side view photograph, I traced off the deck rails, uprights and any other framing and transferred these as a simple line drawing onto a piece of card. The uprights, cut from straight 1mm brass wire (see the K&S Metals stand in your local model shop) were taped to the drawing with tiny pieces of Sellotape. The top rail was added next, from the same material, taped in place and butted against the tops of the uprights. The uprights, incidentally, are extended by about ¼in at the bottom end so that they can be located into holes drilled in the deck.

Using the thinnest of the K&S brass wire, the deck rails and other framing pieces were cut to length and taped in place on top of the uprights, remembering to leave the appropriate gap for the gate. Once the framing was all taped down, it was a simple matter to solder up all the points where wires intersected, thus forming a neat frame unit. An opposite-handed frame was then made up for the other side. The two frames were removed from the card, cleaned up to remove excess solder and then washed under the tap to remove filings, flux etc.

Installing the frames was simply a matter of carefully marking the positions of the uprights, drilling the deck and setting the frames in place. Front and rear top rails were then cut from 1mm wire and a slight curve induced before soldering them to the corners of the side frames. Note how the awning is curved at front and back, but flat in the centre. At this stage, deck, deck houses and boiler were painted in brown.

The awning was cut from 20thou styrene with the positions of the wheelhouse and the cut-out for the ladder marked on top. The latter required careful attention so that it related precisely to the position of the cut-out in the deck house. The ladder was cut from spare 4mm scale signal ladder. Gentle pressure with the fingers induced the slight curve into either end and Evo-Stik secured the awning in place.

At this point I began scouring the shops for suitable ship's fittings – wheel, life belts and engine room vents – and drew a complete blank, unable to find items in the right scale. I made the wheel from a brass clock gear with the teeth filed off and wire handles soldered on, and bent to the engine room vents from solid nickel-silver rod. They were subsequently replaced with white metal castings from RAE Models of Weybridge.

The wheelhouse was a simple styrene assembly job, and the upper railings were made up from brass wire in the same manner as the others. Note the elaborate shaping of the wheelhouse roof, and the bell hung under the eaves (I used an American locomotive bell). The awning was cut carefully to receive the chimney which located in a hole drilled in the boiler top. The canvas valancing around the awning was represented by carefully cut strips of 10thou styrene.

This left the paddle wheel as the main

Below:
The model *Lucy Fisher* with stoker, helmsman and two other crew members. Note the convincing appearance of the louvred sections.

outstanding job to tackle. First, the paddle box. The illustration shows the general arrangement. The sides were cut to shape from 30thou styrene, and the beams which carry the bearings were thickened with a strip of 60thou glued inside. The curved top was formed from 20thou styrene taped to a wooden rolling pin, dunked in boiling water, then cold water, to retain the curve. The paddlebox is slightly narrower than the hull, two lengths of 1mm dia brass wire 'Super glued' to the rear awning upright, forming the braces.

The bearings were tiny pieces of 1/16in diameter brass tube soldered to a piece of brass shim and glued in place on the beams. The paddle shaft is once again 1mm brass wire which revolves in the bearings. At this stage the inside of the paddle box was painted matt black.

The paddle wheel is, in fact, two separate wheels with a bearing in the centre. For my purposes, I omitted this bearing and fitted instead a dummy crank arrangement. The first problem with the paddle wheels is that the very flimsy appearance of the prototype is not practical in a small scale. For my first attempt, I cut rings of styrene sheet and tried installing the ten spokes separately. The result was awful. Using 20thou sheet, I then cut the four wheel sections each as one piece comprising rim, spokes and hub with as much daylight as possible between the spokes. All circular cutting was done with the point of a pair of dividers.

The paddle boards are 4mm wide with the corners nicked out to fit resting on the spokes and around the rim. Care is required to get all the paddle boards on the correct side of the spokes so that the spoke is pushing the board against the water. The styrene dummy crank and some washers form a spacer between the two paddle wheels which were then set on the shaft and the paddlebox gently eased apart until the shaft ends would locate in the bearings.

The deck, deck houses and wheel house are varnished wood finish – I used chocolate brown paint, with matt earth for the deck. Boiler, chimney, and paddle wheels are 'rust' coloured. The hull and deck railings are matt black, with red below the waterline. The awning is off white/fawn, with the upper level railings in white. Names are gilt with red shading. The life belts are the smallest (10mm dia) from the Billing Boats range.

This is certainly the most interesting vessel to appear on this stretch of the Thames in a long time and is a real eye-catcher.

Modelling Canada's 'Silver Lady'

Chris Leigh

In the mid-1980s there are few really 'great' trains left in the world. One of them must surely be the 'Canadian', the former Canadian Pacific streamlined transcontinental passenger train which daily crosses Canada from Toronto/Montreal to Vancouver. Today's 'Canadian' is operated by VIA Rail, the Crown Corporation which, from the late 1970s, took over passenger train operations from both Canadian Pacific and Canadian National. Although there is talk of introducing new bi-level passenger cars, the train is currently formed of ex-CN and CP rolling stock dating from the 1950s headed by General Motors FP9 locomotives of the same vintage.

It is staggering to consider the mileage that this equipment must have run in 30 years of daily crossings of the continent. Indeed, the whole of the transcontinental operation is on a grand scale. A return journey covers all of 6,300 miles and takes a week. When the service was dieselised in the mid-1950s, Canadian Pacific purchased some 155 passenger cars from Budd of Philadelphia, the vast majority of them for the 'Canadian' service. They included dome observation cars, cafeteria dome cars, sleepers, diners and conventional coaches. Initially the stainless steel cars carried the CP maroon letterboard with the name in gold and were headed by FP9s in the maroon and grey colour scheme.

From 1967 CP changed to its corporate image with action red locomotives, coach letterboards to match, and the familiar CP Rail namestyle and 'multimark' logo. It was during this period that generally declining passenger traffic caused the 'Canadian' to be reduced from its original configuration of some 15 cars, to less than half that figure. There was a brief respite in the summer of 1967 when, in connection with the 'Expo 67' World's Fair in Vancouver, the number of dome cars was increased from two to three.

Since the takeover by VIA Rail, the 'Canadian' cars have been refurbished internally to provide a level of comfort which is distinct luxury by most modern standards. Externally the train has been somewhat spoiled by the garish VIA Rail blue livery applied to the locomotives and the mixture of ex-CP stainless steel cars with ex-CN blue and yellow painted vehicles. Nevertheless, the demise of the 'Super Continental' on the parallel ex-CN route in 1981 has led to strengthening of the 'Canadian' such that it is not unusual to see four FP9s heading over the Kicking Horse pass with 17 cars in tow.

From the modelling point of view the 'Canadian' in pre-VIA days makes an impressive train and for my money it looked fine in the 'action red' livery,

Left:
The westbound 'Canadian' descends from the Kicking Horse Pass behind three VIA Rail passenger units assisted, in the lead, by a Canadian Pacific SD40-2 freight locomotive. From the front, the coaches are ex-CP baggage dormitory, ex-CP coach, ex-CN 'Dayniter', ex-CP skyline dome/coffee shop and another ex-CN 'Dayniter'. The ex-CN cars are in painted blue livery. Photographed 8 September 1983. *B. Denton*

Since its incorporation into VIA Rail, the 'Canadian' is no longer an all-stainless steel consist, some blue-painted ex-CN vehicles being included. Summer services may load to more than 16 cars, requiring four 1,750hp diesels to lift them over the Rockies. On 28 August 1981, the westbound 'Canadian' is seen at Johnson Creek, with Mount Eisenhower in the background, next stop Lake Louise. As always a 'Park' class tail-dome sleeper brings up the rear, in this case, *Revelstoke Park*. *Chris Leigh*

Bound for Vancouver, CP Rail-liveried FP9A No 1413 leads two GP9s at the head of the 'Canadian' entering Banff, Alberta on 29 August 1981. A VIA Rail porter brings up the baggage ready for loading. *Chris Leigh*

although I can well understand the feelings of those who prefer the softer ambience of the maroon era. For my purposes the action red era offered another modelling advantage in that a six or seven car formation is better suited for modelling – with 85ft cars and three locomotives the train is still eight or nine feet long! Film buffs will recall the excellent Gene Wilder film *Silver Streak* in which a short formation of 'Canadian' cars and locomotives thinly disguised with bogus 'Amroad' stickers played the title role. With exhibition appearances in mind, here was a train which many of the non-railway public might readily identify.

The FP7 and FP9 locomotives used on the 'Canadian' are not readily available in ready-to-run model form but the similar (slightly shorter) F7 and F9 are available from a variety of manufacturers and are generally accepted by North American modellers for passenger train use. I use a three-unit lash-up of Athearn F7s having a cabless 'B' unit flanked on either side by an 'A' unit. The more powerful F9 type is available in the Bachmann range.

The Athearn F7 is available in CP Rail action red livery but does need some attention to the body in order to make it correct for Canadian practice. My units are fitted with the Walthers detail kit and one 'A' unit has winterisation hood and icicle breakers fitted. I also filled the lower front headlight, fitted new horns and applied black and white striping to the inner ends of each unit. The leading unit is powered with the Athearn flywheel mechanism, while the trailing dummy 'A' unit is fitted with a GSB cab interior. It is my intention at some time to fit constant lighting, probably by using batteries installed inside the 'B' unit.

The rake of model coaches has been developed gradually and still has some way to go before I am happy with it. I started with standard Athearn streamlined vehicles repainted to suit. However there is no tail-dome car in the Athearn range and most of the other vehicles are under scale length and of incorrect window layout for the 'Canadian'. The first step in upgrading the train was the acquisition of a Con-cor tail dome car, followed subsequently by other Con-cor vehicles. Most of the vehicles in

Below:
The 'Canadian' at Cobden, Ontario in July 1976. Leading is FP9 locomotive No 1410 in CP Rail action red livery. The icicle breakers and winterisation hoods can be seen, as can the different front lighting arrangement from US diesels. *K. A. Gansel*

this range are still not correct for the 'Canadian' but they do provide a basis for conversion. They are also, in most cases, of the correct scale 85ft length.

When I rode on the 'Canadian' in 1981 from Banff through to Vancouver, I finally became convinced of the need to improve my models and to try and scratch together a train that was a little more representative of the prototype. I began with the tail dome car. The Con-cor model is close to correct in outline and the window layout is correct for the 'Canadian', although the spacing on one side is slightly adrift. The model has no interior fittings or tail sign, but does have a large 'Rio-Grande Zephyr'-style rear light which is not present on the CPR cars.

Dismantling the Con-cor model entails separating the roof from the body by levering gently on the clips in the underside of the floor. These enable the integral roof and glazing to be withdrawn.

With this car I planned to install an interior in the dome section and the rear lounge, and to fit an illuminated tail sign. The 'Park' class tail-dome cars on the 'Canadian' contain sleeping accommodation, two lounges – the Mural lounge and the tail lounge, and the dome observation section. The corridor floor on the left of the car (looking towards the front of the train) is lowered between the bogies to allow standing clearance below the upper deck. This lowered section is denoted by a body fairing on the lower side of the car, but the rest of the fairing on the Con-cor model must be cut and filed away.

The lighted tail-sign is one of a range produced by Tomar Industries in the USA. It consists of the tail-sign (a section of colour slide film), mounting box and diffuser, a miniature filament bulb, and the necessary diodes and 'ballast' bulb to provide constant brightness for the sign.

I must admit that I set out on the wrong foot with this kit and I really did have a lot of trouble. I wanted to fit the lighting equipment below the false floor of my interior unit, so I installed self-adhesive copper foil tape in place of wiring. The diodes for the constant brightness unit fitted neatly in a recess in the Con-cor floor and I followed precisely the wiring instructions. The unit operates with a 1.5V

Below:
An artist's impression which portrays accurately the interior of one of the Skyline dome/coffee shop cars, with the stairs to the dome visible in the centre. Beneath the dome is a kitchen, with the corridor visible on the right.
Canadian Pacific

Extremes of Garden Railway Motive Power running on Gauge 1 Track

This picture:
A diminutive vertical-boilered De Winton 0-4-0T which uses some Mamod parts seen on Dave Pinniger's AVR. *Chris Leigh*

Bottom:
At the other end of the scale is Allen Levy's Aster 'Big Boy' 4-8-8-4 seen here on the outdoor tracks of the London Toy and Model Museum.
Chris Leigh

miniature bulb in the tail sign itself, a 'ballast' bulb being used to absorb the excess power. This bulb is quite large and was fitted inside one of the sleeping compartments. Phosphor bronze wiper pick-ups were fitted to both trucks, rubbing on the axles, and soldered to the brass screws which I had installed in place of the Con-cor bogie-pivot pins.

With track power applied, the unit worked tolerably well and the tail sign lit with an even glow. However, the first sign of trouble was that the body of the car became very warm around the area of the ballast bulb – so warm that there was a risk of the plastic body distorting. To reduce this risk I wrapped the bulb in aluminium foil. Actually running the unit with a locomotive produced more problems. The locomotive, normally very smooth and reliable, took off in series of violent jerks, accompanied by the most alarming pyrotechnic display and sound effects from under the coach.

Assuming that I had made some mistake, I stopped the test and took the roof off the passenger car. I had forgotten all about the heat generated by the ballast bulb until I accidentally touched the exposed bulb. The resultant burn convinced me to remove the unit entirely and formulate some other arrangement, but not before I noticed that the 1.5V

miniature bulb appeared to have burnt out.

I must assume that the excessive heating of the ballast bulb and the subsequent failure of the miniature bulb were the result of some mistake I had made in wiring up, but a check of the instructions failed to reveal what this might be.

In the end, I settled for retaining the bogie pick-ups and installing a standard 12V bulb behind the tail sign. This, of course, does not provide constant brilliance since the light level varies according to the track voltage. Nevertheless, it does seem to provide a more practical arrangement. Perhaps someone like Polytechnic will, in due course, devise a suitable system using modern electronics which would function in this particular application.

The only changes to the body of the car involved cutting away the fairing between the bogies and removing the large tail light. The hole left by the latter was filled with Plastic Padding, filed smooth, and sprayed over with Humbrol silver paint.

The dome interior was built up on a floor of 60thou styrene sheet, cut to fit inside the aperture in the car roof. The dome is arranged much like the seating on a 'lowbridge'-type bus. The centre aisle allows sufficient headroom for an average

Left:
'Park' class tail dome/observation car *Laurentide Park* with the 'Canadian' CP Rail drumhead on the rear door, at Ottawa in 1978. *K. A. Gansel*

Below:
The Con-Cor model with the rear door modified and the Tomar drumhead installed. *Author*

passenger to stand, but the floor at either side is raised so that one steps up to reach the seats. These are arranged in six forward-facing rows, two seats on either side of the aisle. Access is by a short staircase from the rear lounge. I used some cast white metal seats, cut to fit and built up the remaining interior parts from styrene sheet. When fitting passengers it is important to realise that the overscale thickness of the dome glazing reduces the headroom by a large amount. It is thus necessary to cut the figures to fit, or to use underscale (TT) figures.

The lower deck interior floor and partitions were also built up from 60thou styrene sheet. The rear lounge arm chairs were cut down white metal seat castings. The stairs were built up from 30thou styrene sheet, with the built-in writing desk adjacent.

A Kadee coupler was fitted to the floor at the rear of the car, whilst at the leading end, the coupler mounting bar was cut short and a Kadee draft-gear box glued in place. The coupling fitted in this way enables the vehicles to be close coupled but still negotiate the tightest available curve (2ft).

The next Con-cor vehicle to be tackled was the dining car. This model has the smooth roof which must be replaced with a fluted roof as fitted to most other Con-cor vehicles. I arranged a straight swap with another vehicle, but it is understood that both roof types are available separately to facilitate such changes. The CP dining cars have a long blank section on the side where the kitchen provisioning door is located. Rather than attempt to fill several windows, I cut the windows section at this end of the car away, filed the edges smooth and fitted a piece of 60thou styrene with one small window aperture. On the opposite side of the car (in the corridor alongside the kitchen) two small windows required filling with styrene sheet and filing smooth. When these modifications were complete, the affected areas were sprayed in with silver paint. Interior detail has yet to be added in the dining saloon.

Any further conversions will necessitate cutting out the window area of the Con-cor vehicles completely and replacing them with a styrene insert having the correct window formation cut out. In this way it is hoped to produce baggage-dormitory, standard coach, and 'Chateau' or 'Manor' class sleeping cars. The other dome car is not quite right, but conversion would not be easy so I have opted to let this one pass as it is and simply fit an interior.

Left:
The 'Canadian' in a typical CP Rail configuration. The coaches are, from the rear, 'Park' tail dome, 'Manor' sleeper, 'Chateau' sleeper, diner, 'Manor' sleeper, two 'Chateau' sleepers, 'Skyline' dome, two coaches, baggage/dormitory.
CP Rail

Below:
The model, *Banff Park*, with interior fitted, awaiting removal of the valance between the trucks.
Author

Hengaeau

Above:
A quiet moment at Porthmeir Harbour on the 009 narrow gauge layout of D. E. Anning. Hengaeau is based on Welsh narrow gauge practice.

Above:
Prince crosses the bridge at Hafody Llyn with a train of vintage four-wheelers.   *Both: Len Weal*

41

Two views on D. E. Anning's Welsh narrow gauge layout,
Hengaeau, which was featured in *Model Railway
Constructor* September 1984. *Photographs:* Len Weal

Great Eastern Tram Locomotives

All photographs from the Real
Photographs catalogue

Continued on page 46

**One of the 0-6-0T tram locomotives,
No 138, built in 1908 and seen here
in GER brown and blue livery.**
(64217)

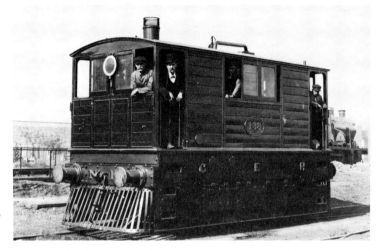

**Seen standing at Upwell with a
passenger tram for Wisbech is one
of the earlier 0-4-0T locomotives, No
127, built at Stratford in 1892.**
(64172)

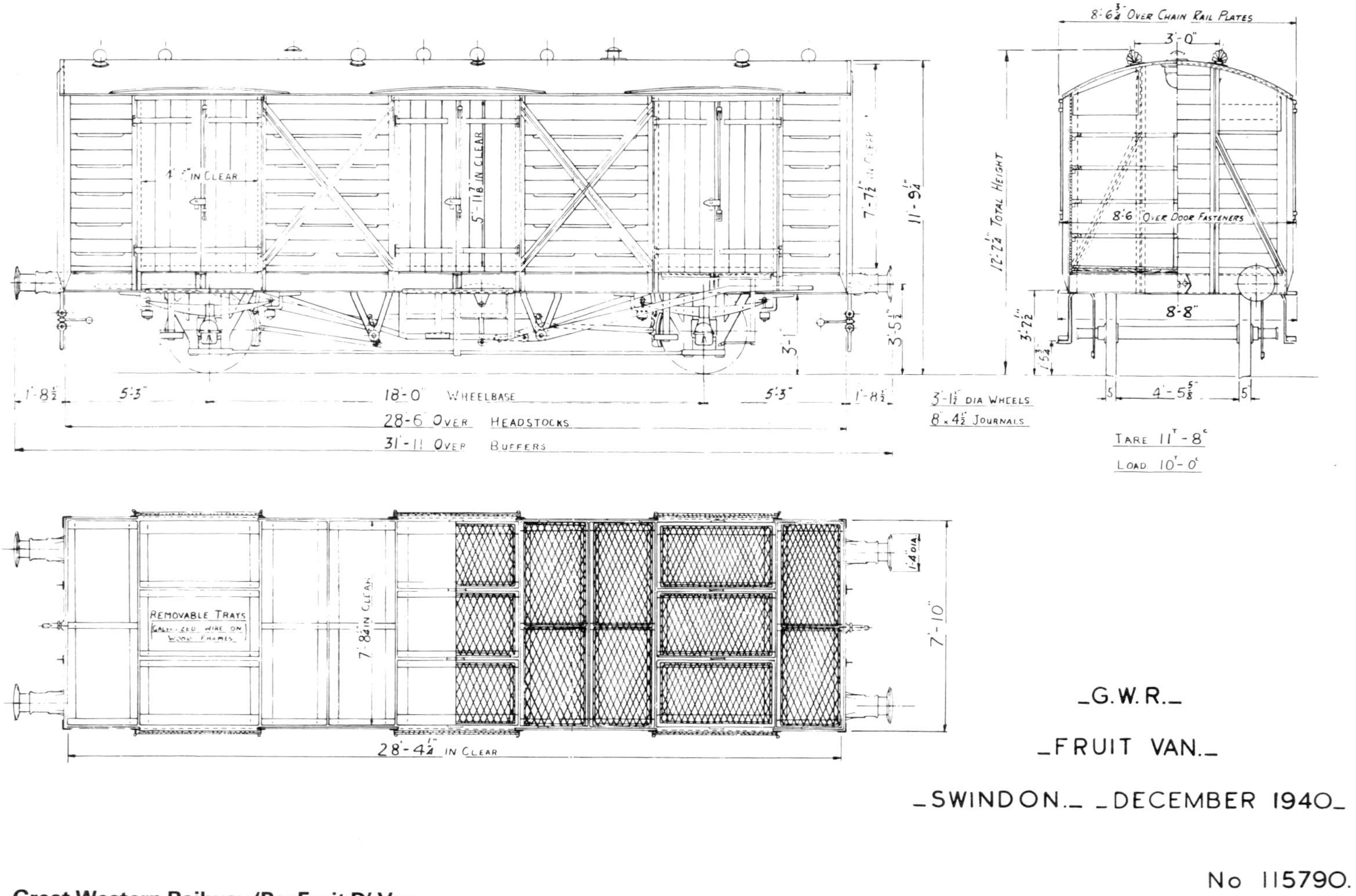

8'·6¾" Over Chain Rail Plates

3'·0"

8'·6" Over Door Fasteners

8'·8"

4'·5⅝"

Tare 11ᵀ·8ᶜ
Load 10'·0ᶜ

3'·1"

12'·2⅞" Total Height

3'·7⅞"

3'·1⅛" Dia Wheels
8'·4½" Journals

11'·9¾"

3'·5½"

7'·7½" In Clear

1'·1¼"

5'·3"

3'·1"

18'·0" Wheelbase

28'·6" Over Headstocks

31'·1½" Over Buffers

5'·11¾" In Clear

1'·¾" In Clear

5'·3"

1'·8½"

7'·10"

1" dia.

28'·4½" In Clear

7'·8½" In Clear

7'·8½" In Clear

REMOVABLE TRAYS
Small Ø Wire on
Iron Frames

–G.W.R.–

–FRUIT VAN.–

–SWINDON.– –DECEMBER 1940–

No 115790.

Great Western Railway 'PasFruit D' Van

Above: See article on page 6.
No B875266, a BR-built GWR-design Fruit van. The plain
plywood end and doors contrast with the ventilated third.
planked side which has slatted louvres in the upper
Notice how the lettering at both ends is positioned by the
diagonal strapping. Photographed in Southampton docks
during April 1969. *Paul W. Bartlett*

Below:
No B875800, a BR-built Fruit van, its similarity to the
standard box van is obvious, and only the addition of pocket
ventilators distinguishes it. This example had no branding
when seen at Kidderminster in July 1973 and the number is
placed unusually high up on the side. *Paul W. Bartlett*

As LNER Class 'J70' and carrying its 1924 number, 7137 shunts at Wisbech with end doors and sideplates open. *(R6151)*

A number of the 'J70' 0-6-0Ts had their sideplates removed when not allocated to tramway duties. No 8219 in the LNER 1946 renumbering is seen in this condition. *(R8067)*

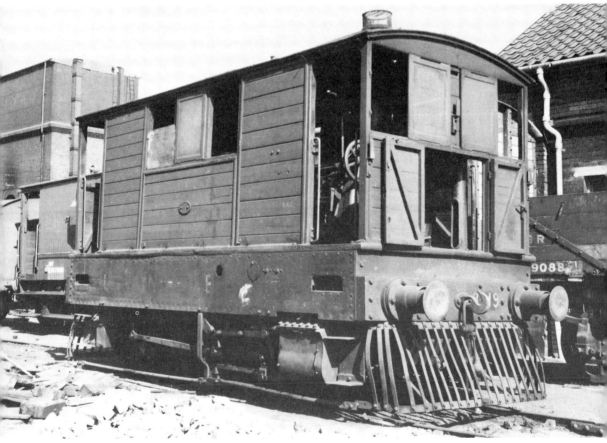

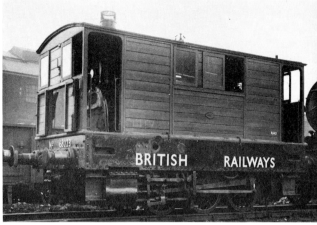

Above left:
Ex-works in LNER 1924 livery, No 7126 is devoid of sideplates and cowcatchers but retains the side chains on the buffer beam.

Above:
Class J70 No 68223 in original British Railways livery with black frames and brown woodwork. Sideplates and cowcatchers were subsequently refitted and this locomotive was among the last to work on the Wisbech & Upwell, being withdrawn in 1955. *(R5173)*

Left:
Nearing the end of its days, a 'J70' in final BR livery, running with parts of the side plating removed. *(K2052)*

Below left:
The end of the road for a 'J70' stripped of its rods and motion and awaiting breaking up. *(K2806)*

Improving a Pannier

P. Harrison

Some elementary detailing for a Hornby model

Introduction

The beginning of the long break last Christmas found me at home with a rare opportunity to carry out some modelling on consecutive days rather than intermittent weekends. Looking around at the various projects which I plan to do, my eye came to rest on the Hornby 8750 class pannier tank which had been earmarked for a repaint for several years. I decided that, coupled with some elementary detailing, this would provide a suitably straightforward and none too taxing exercise for the time of year!

The Options Available

The Hornby model dates from 1972, and while it is quite an acceptable model with a few minor dimensional errors, its age does tend to show alongside more recent models. From 1981 a more realistic appearance was provided by means of a painted finish, albeit in a simplified form with too much green and not enough black. My version was years old and so predated this improvement, being

Below:
The completed model, repainted, detailed and fitted with brake gear.

in self-coloured plastic of a rather vivid green almost everywhere! I began the job by examining the model and comparing it with the details in *A Pictorial Record of Great Western Engines Volume 2* by J. H. Russell. The following list was the result:

The locomotive had a tapered chimney, but that on the model is straight.

Below:
The cab and bunker showing fire irons, brackets, vacuum pipe, window guards and handrails.

Some were without topfeed, but the model has it. Tank fillers seem more circular than those modelled, which are elongated.

Top of safety valve cover moulding is plain. Cab windows too small back and front; rear windows had guard irons.

Whistles were not both the same size.

Pipework beneath the tanks in front of the cab was more prominent, as was the pipework running up the sides on to the tank tops.

Bunker steps and high level vertical handrail on the left hand side only.

Remove moulded handrails and tool iron brackets and fit separate wire ones.

Remove moulded smokebox door handle and replace.

Provide lamp bracket and lamps.

Pipes run along the edge of both footplates.

Tank vents modelled as pips instead of mushrooms.

Model has no bufferbeam detail.

Buffers should be parallel shank, not tapered.

Provide brake gear and front sandboxes.

Open out top cab steps (access to rear sandboxes).

Coupling rods overthick.

The 57XX variant was similar, except that it had the lower, flatter cab roof, and is modelled by Mainline. Not all of this list was tackled as the basic model was neither dead scale nor very expensive and I wanted to keep in proportion the standard of extra detail, time and expense incurred.

Body Detailing

Having removed the body from the chassis I set to work removing the unwanted detail. The tank top and part of the cab front is a separate moulding which should be stuck to the rest of the body but in my model was not, so I was able to remove it, thereby making the work easier. The safety valve cover and whistles are a push fit and may easily be removed. In the event I decided not to attempt any detailing on the top of the safety valve cover – mainly because I could not think of any method which I was sure would achieve the desired result! One whistle was shortened by filing (it is a piece of metal). The chimney was left untouched as I felt the discrepancy was not significant enough to warrant the cost and difficult amputation and replacement. Likewise the filler caps remained, as I was not certain of the actual shape, but they did receive screw locks formed from fine plastic rodding. The tank vents however were replaced using Westward

Scale Model castings. The moulded handrails were pared off, as were the fire iron brackets and unwanted steps on the bunker, and the cabside numberplates.

The cab windows were the largest single item of work on the body. Their small size is primarily due to the thickness of the moulding in the cab side, and the simplified line adopted in the tank top moulding. Using a flat file, the lower edge of the front windows was lowered approximately 1mm until level with the top of the firebox. The outer sides and top edge were widened until just over 1mm thickness remained at the face. In the case of the top this cuts into the roof only slightly, but the sides are some 3mm thick so that it is necessary to chamfer the edge (see sketch). For the rear windows similar treatment is required, although the lower edge is now correct and a little has to be removed from the inside edge. The chamfer is disguised at the painting stage by applying Brunswick green only to the outer face, and black to the inside of the cab and window edges. This renders it virtually undetectable in the front, especially if crew are fitted inside the body partially to obscure the motor block. For the rear windows the illusion is completed by the addition of bars to protect the

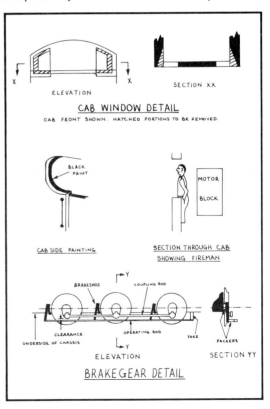

CAB WINDOW DETAIL

CAB FRONT SHOWN. HATCHED PORTIONS TO BE REMOVED.

ELEVATION

SECTION XX

BLACK PAINT

CAB SIDE PAINTING

MOTOR BLOCK

SECTION THROUGH CAB SHOWING FIREMAN

BRAKESHOE   COUPLING ROD

CLEARANCE   OPERATING ROD   YOKE

UNDERSIDE OF CHASSIS

PACKERS

ELEVATION

SECTION YY

BRAKEGEAR DETAIL

Above:
An ex-L&Y 'Pug' 0-4-0ST in industrial livery by Bill Hunt of Farnborough Railway Enthusiasts Club. *W. G. Hunt*

Below:
An ex-LBSCR 'K' class 2-6-0 from a Mallard Models 4mm scale kit, running on the Farnborough REC Alton layout.

Marking the 150th anniversary of the Great Western Railway, a DH89 Dragon Rapide was to be repainted in Railway Air Services livery to record the part played by the GWR in establishing internal air services. This Heller 1:72 scale model was hand-painted into RAS livery, see the article on page 121. *Chris Leigh*

glass (etched brass by Crownline). I decided not to glaze the windows as I felt this might make the chamfering more noticeable.

The reduction stage was completed by removal of the buffer shanks and 'hook' moulding from the bufferbeam, and opening a square hole above the upper cab step.

Reconstruction began by fixing the tank top into the body and then adding pipes along each side of the footplate (one for steam, one for vacuum – not all of the class had these, Nos 6700-49 for example were unfitted) and also up the tank sides and across the top just in front of the cab. Fine plastic rod was used for the pipework, as it was for lamp irons – one above each buffer and one each slightly offset from centre in front of the chimney and above the coupling at the front; and one slightly off centre in the rear of the bunker top. These were glued into small holes. A similar approach provided the new smokebox handle – an 'L' shaped piece was fixed into the centre, and a shorter piece glued to it and the smokebox door. Two sandboxes were fabricated from double thicknesses of 80thou Plastikard and filed to shape before fitting beneath the footplate at the front, while moulding pips from a kit furnished the circular fillers above the footplate. Small pieces of wire were bent to shape to form the fire iron brackets on the rear of the bunker, to which I later fixed a bucket and fire irons (white metal castings by Springside).

Wire was also used to form the new handrails. Although they are overscale, I used turned brass handrail knobs wherever there were knobs, as I feel

their appearance more than compensates. These were pre-painted black before fixing with a small amount of Superglue. Holes were drilled to accept the handrails which fixed directly to the body.

On the bufferbeams I fitted turned brass parallel shank buffers, vacuum pipes and etched brass coupling hooks. Unfortunately it was not possible to fit the steam pipes and screw couplings as these would have fouled the tension lock coupling. The only remaining bodywork item was the pipework beneath the tank in front of the cab. This is a relief moulding on the Hornby model and I decided not to attempt to replace it as I felt it unlikely that I would achieve an appearance which repaid the necessary work. On the left hand side I intended to place a couple of spare lamps which would obscure the mouldings further.

The body was now ready for painting. A repaint alone would have considerably improved the appearance – a black running plate for example makes the model seem longer and lower. Basically the tank top, sides and front, cab, bunker, toolboxes and splasher fronts are Brunswick green. Everything else is black. I also used black paint to disguise infill areas on the moulding – on the vertical plastic behind the splashers which hides the motor, on the plastic behind the toolboxes above the splashers and on the inner half of the cabside moulding (see sketch). The effect on the cabside is to reduce the apparent thickness of the moulding, which was later enhanced by the provision of a fireman (also helping to hide the motor block) who was filed below the waist so that the upper half of his body overhung the side as far as the green paint, so seeming to stand inside the cab. The safety valve cover was given a coat of brass paint before refitting to the body and the chimney copper capped. Wire handrails were then fitted and painted black before

applying Great Western transfers to the tank sides, and route availability and power classification to the cab sides. The whistles were replaced, with the shorter one on the left hand side. Finally the bodywork was completed by the provision of two spare lamps, a headlamp (on the bunker top for a change), a bucket and fire iron on the brackets, cabside numberplates and the number on the front bufferbeam only.

Chassis Detailing

On the chassis there was little to be done. I began by replacing the Hornby couplings by smaller Mainline ones (on tight curves this might present problems because the parallel buffers are slightly longer than the original tapered ones). Small adjustments were necessary on both couplings to fit the chassis block. At the front this was simply to remove a little plastic from the side, but at the rear the back of the coupling moulding has to be removed completely and the spring retained by fixing a piece of Plastikard to the bottom of the chassis, extending under the spring.

The brake gear was built up using white metal castings by Springside. Each brake shoe should be in front of the wheel, with its centre line on the centre line of the axle. To bring the shoes into line with the wheels, small pieces of 80thou Plastikard were used as packing – a small hole being drilled to accept the pip in the white metal casting. I found it easier to fix the casting to the packing, and then the packing to the chassis (once again using Superglue). Occasionally it was necessary gently to scratch the blackening of the chassis block in order to give the adhesive a key. The front shoes were fitted first, with a piece of 40thou plastic rod between their lower ends beneath the coupling to strengthen them (which also represents part of the brake gear). The lower end of the casting should be below the lowest point of the coupling rod movement but check it now! A 1mm strip of 20thou Plastikard was cut to form the operating bar. To allow for sideplay in the wheels I offset this strip by using a 1.5mm packing piece of the same size between the bottom of the casting and the operating bar. At the rear the bar is supported on a yoke of 40thou Plastikard fixed beneath the block, which was notched in the centre so it does not protrude any further than the existing cog wheel. Finally the last two castings are fitted on each side attaching them to the chassis at the top and the operating bar at the bottom.

The Hornby coupling rods can be removed and gently filed to produce the thinner, slightly fish-bellied shape. This eats into the fluting so the face must also be filed smooth. I made no attempt to reduce the size of the rod around the pins and screws.

The last item which could be undertaken on the chassis is the provision of guard irons, but I decided against this as there is already a lot of detail in this area at the front (coupling and brake gear) while at the rear it is obscured by the cab steps.

Conclusion

You can judge for yourself how effective the detailing has been. I feel that the detailed model stands up to comparison with current production models quite well, and yet the work involved is neither too difficult nor extensive. Finally, the cost of the extra components was well under £5.

Below:
An '87XX' series 0-6-0PT with the earlier pattern cab.
Real Photographs

Diesel Fleet for Western Canada

CP Rail SD40-2 No 5647 is a modified and repainted Athearn model. It is seen posed on a short section of track using natural light and the real sky for background. *Chris Leigh*

British Columbia Railway's most recent acquisition in 1981 was SD40-2 No 762, here seen at North Vancouver. This example has the larger 'snoot' nose which can be modelled using a Cannon Prototype Replicas kit. No 762 was one of a batch of 12, two of which were written off in a wreck in 1984 and which are to be replaced by five more delivered in the new red, white and blue livery. *Chris Leigh*

Diesel fleet for Western Canada

R. Borchardt, K. R. Willows
and Chris Leigh

I once commented in *MRC* about the plight of modellers, in this country and in North America, who were seeking models for genuine Canadian prototypes. The response was interesting, for while most modellers considered that I was correct in stating that there was little pure Canadian material readily available, one retailer considered that the market was well covered. However, the fact remains that without a major Canadian manufacturer in the business, the number of ready-to-run Canadian models remains limited.

However, the situation has improved in some respects, and far more models are now appearing in Canadian colours. The MDC Roundhouse range, for instance now includes freight cars and passenger vehicles in Canadian National and Canadian Pacific colours, plus freight stock in Pacific Great Eastern, British Columbia Railway and Ontario Northland

Below:
The authors, Bob Borchardt (left) and Keith Willows (right) with Chris Leigh, operating a pair of VIA Rail 'F' units on the Fraser Canyon layout.

liveries. Some diesel locomotives have also been released in CP, CN and BCR liveries but these have been models in the Atlas, Bachmann and Model-Power ranges, all of which are intended primarily for the US market. Canadian diesel locomotives incorporate several prominent detail differences from their US counterparts, while the 'buy Canadian' policy of the railways north of the 49th parallel has meant that many locomotives are US designs built in Canada and therefore have further design changes. This article suggests some ways in which the US model diesels can be simply brought into keeping with Canadian practice.

To any newcomer, the North American diesel scene is rather like trying to find the way out of a maze while blindfolded. The major diesel locomotive manufacturers each produced numerous different models, often allocating a new design number when only minor changes had been made. Sometimes, outwardly similar locomotives incorporate different engines or equipment resulting in a new design number or a suffix to the original designation. North of the border, these numbers are further complicated because the railways have their own classification system which largely ignores the makers' designations. In addition, the CP, CN, and BCR systems are all different. Thus, the Alco Century 630, a 3,000hp Co-Co design produced by Alco's Canadian successors Montreal Locomotive Works under the MLW M-630 model number is an MF30a on the CN, a DRF-30c on CP Rail and an RS 30 on the British Columbia Railway. In the CN system the first letter indicates the manufacturer and the second the purpose (freight, passenger or switcher). The numerical section, common to all the systems indicates horsepower, in this case, 3,000hp. The suffix letter indicates a delivery group (a = first batch, c = third batch, etc) while the CP system initials simply indicate the purpose – diesel road freight. Similarly the BCR classification means, road switcher 3,000hp, although latterly their system has changed to come in line with that of Canadian National.

The Canadian diesel modeller has one great advantage over his steam counterpart. There are few inexpensive ready-to-run models of Canadian steam locomotives, and even the celebrated 'Royal

Below:
British Columbia Railway RS-18 No 606 shunting a maintenance-of-way train in Lillooet yard. In HO a reasonable representation can be made by modifying the Model Power RS-11. *Chris Leigh*

Above:
Wearing the classic CN striped livery, F9A and B units from Bachmann and Athearn, head the 'Super Continental' passenger train over the Anderson Creek trestle. On the lower level a Canfor SW1200RS, described in *MRC Annual 1984,* **heads a logging train.** *Chris Leigh*

Below:
Another view of Anderson Creek on the Fraser Canyon layout. Keith Willows' modified Athearn SW1200 is on the lower level, while a rare British Columbia Railway M630 with 'comfort cab' from a Model Power item heads an oil train over the trestle. *Chris Leigh*

Hudson' which must rank among the world's most beautiful locomotives, is only available as a limited production Japanese brass model priced well beyond the means of many of us. The diesel fan can take many of the US types, which have the advantage of very reasonable price tags, and can produce a representative fleet. The details below are not intended to be in any way exhaustive and in the main they reflect the conversions done by us for the Egham & Staines Model Railway Society's Fraser Canyon layout.

General Motors F7 & F9

These are the most familiar North American locomotives, the main difference between them being an extra ventilator aft of the cab door on the F9. The passenger versions, FP7 and FP9 are slightly longer. They are used in Canada by CN and CP and by Ontario Northland. Most of those that were in passenger service on the CN and CP lines are now owned by VIA Rail Canada, the government organisation which has taken over the passenger services of the two national systems.

Models of F9 and F7 are available from Bachmann and Athearn respectively. The latter also produces the cabless 'B' unit version and non-powered dummy units. The classic formation of these units was two cabless units between two with cabs (A-B-B-A) for passenger service, and since the models are quite powerful this can be represented with one powered unit and three dummies. However, even on the heavy trans-Continental trains, A-B, A-B-B or A-B-A formations are not uncommon and CP Rail was quite prone to supplement such formations with a GP9 type freight locomotive. As with some of the

British diesel classes, GP9s are in service with and without steam generators for passenger service. No ready-to-run FP7 or FP9s are available so one must make do with the freight version.

Both the Athearn and Bachmann F units have the double headlights favoured in the USA, and for Canadian practice the lower light must be removed and the hole filled with Plastic Padding and filed smooth. The F unit detail kit produced by Walthers provides glazing for all windows in the Athearn model, together with all necessary handrails. A highly detailed cab interior kit for this type is produced by GSB Rail.

Athearn produce their F unit in CP Rail 'action red' livery and CN green and yellow and I believe that Bachmann may have covered the CN black and white livery. Canadian modellers will need to pay most attention to the top details on this type. CN units require a roof-mounted bell and horns, and CP units have only the horns (the obligatory bell is often concealed on CP locomotives). Both railways have fitted winterisation equipment to enable the units to operate more efficiently in the extreme cold of a Canadian winter. This equipment consists of a box-shaped ventilator over the cooling system fans. The ventilator can be closed in order to return warm air to the engine air-intakes. The CP and CN winterisation hoods differ in shape and it is best to refer to photographs of a specific locomotive. In addition, CN units have extra plumbing in connection with their system. The CP winterisation hood is generally a prominent tall structure, and can be built up with styrene sheet. Canadian Pacific's trans-continental train 'The Canadian' conveyed several of the Budd dome observation cars in its formation and to prevent the glazing in the domes

Left:
CP Rail Baldwin switcher No 7072 and a couple of sister locomotives are among the last of their type working for a class 1 railroad anywhere in North America. No 7072 and a very tatty example in the background were [Athearn's S-12 switcher makes a good start for modelling this type]. Photographed in 1981 at Nanaimo on Vancouver Island. *Chris Leigh*

being smashed by icicles hanging in tunnels, locomotives assigned to this service were often fitted with icicle breakers. These consisted of three metal frames mounted on the roof and shaped to the loading gauge of the dome cars. Not all CP F units were so equipped and those passed to VIA have had the icicle breakers removed, as high freight cars now break the icicles.

Many F units on both CN and CP are fitted with rock or ditch lights. These are small high powered lights mounted low down on the front end to assist in spotting rock falls or other obstructions on the track or in tunnels. Some CP units also had a lighting unit situated in the centre of the roof. Two details of painting are worth mentioning here. The black and white stripes on the sides of CN F units slope down toward the front on both sides and are angled at 30deg to the horizontal. Most other CN

locomotives in this colour scheme have 45deg stripes sloping down to the right on both sides. In the CP 'action red' scheme the front of the locomotive has white stripes on red, while the rear (always the end with the black and white multimark logo) is striped in white on black. Most commercially available models have both ends painted red and white.

General Motors GP-40

This is a useful type operated by CN and also by the Government of Ontario (GO) commuter system. It is a 3,000hp Bo-Bo, first produced in 1965. Models in HO scale are available from Atlas and Bachmann. CN had examples painted in both the black and white striped scheme and the earlier all black with the 'lazy 3' CN logo.

Left:
CP Rail GP-9 No 8520 is mechanically similar to the FP-9 to which it is coupled, the 'geeps' being general purpose locomotives rather than passenger types. No 8520 is fitted with steam heating, the water being carried in a tank between the bogies which in turn means moving the long cylindrical air tanks onto the roof. This example has dynamic brakes and a winterisation hood. *J. Jones*

Below:
A pair of Athearn GP-9s modified to represent Nos 8833 and 8676 as seen running on Vancouver Island in 1976. No 8833 was still in early CP maroon and grey livery. Extra fittings include rerailing ramps, horns and bells.

Above:
An original SD40 CN No 5092 was adapted by Bob
Borchardt from an AHM ready-to-run model. It is here seen
crossing the Jaws of Death bridge on Egham & Staines
Model Railway Society's Fraser Canyon layout. *Chris Leigh*

The numbers of Alco/MLW RS-3s in traffic are steadily diminishing. This CPR pair have been modified for hump shunting and the leading unit has had its short hood cut down. *B. Denton*

The GP-40s used by GO Transit show a number of interesting variations. They are used for push-pull commuter services with a non-powered F unit providing cab facilities at the opposite end of the train. More recent deliveries have been classified GP-40TC and these are slightly longer and incorporate train control equipment for operation from a driving trailer coach. The GO GP-40s are not equipped with dynamic braking, so the flaired radiators on the long hood of the model must be removed together with the circular top radiator. Some locomotives have a snow-hood covering the radiators immediately behind the cab, and these can be added from styrene sheet.

In common with Canadian practice since the mid-seventies, later GO GP-40s are fitted with the crew comfort cab devised by CN and the rail unions. This affords considerably greater standards of comfort and safety for locomotive crews and results in a vastly changed appearance to the locomotive. It will be no secret that Chris Leigh has marketed a cast white metal kit for this cab, which can be simply grafted on to the cut-down body of either the Atlas or Bachmann types.

General Motors GP-38

This is outwardly similar to the GP-40 and is operated by both CP and CN. It is available in HO in the Atlas range in both high and low short hood versions. The high short hood version is produced in CN livery, which is a pity since CN does not have the high hood version. Recent production GP-38s have been modified and updated and the design classified GP-38-2 ('dash 2'), a model of this version being available from Life-Like. The 'dash 2' is also used by both CN and CP, while the former also has some with comfort cabs. I altered the Atlas model to the comfort cab version and fitted ditch lights, bell, horns and snow plough. However, to be strictly correct, the dynamic brake radiators should also have been removed.

General Motors SD-40

Canadian modellers will have welcomed the HO model from AHM/Mehanoteknika. The examples supplied in undecorated pale grey plastic take an air-brushed paint finish superbly. The SD-40, a six-axle 3,000hp giant is the most widely used diesel locomotive in Canada. The majority of them are 'dash 2' versions which are on a longer underframe than the standard version, as now produced by Athearn. The AHM model represents the earlier version and it would not be an easy job to stretch the underframe.

The standard SD-40 is operated by both CP and CN in limited numbers and for these the model needs little alteration. The two lights in the centre above the windscreen must be replaced by a bell on a short bracket, and two new lights provided in the front of the low hood. I used some 1/16in dia. brass tube for the light mountings and fitted each with a small jewel. Jewels were also fitted above the front number boards, as marker lights.

A brake wheel is fitted to the left side of the low hood, and a rerailer is carried in typical position behind the cab. I unclipped the bogie frames in order to paint the wheel centres black, and added a wire speedo cable to the centre axlebox of the leading truck. For spray painting the model is ideal. The cab roof and glazing unclip, and the body is a separate moulding from the underframe and walkways. There are four screws holding the body in place (two hidden by the front truck) and once these are removed the fuel tank can be withdrawn and the body lifted off.

The SD40-2 is now produced by both GSB Rail and Athearn. Chris Leigh's conversion of the Athearn model to a CPR example was described in MRC July 1983. Canadian National operates many examples with the crew comfort cab for which Canadian Prototype Replicas and Chris Leigh both produced kits. The BCR examples have the longer 'snoot' short hood containing remote control equipment.

Montreal Locomotive Works M-630

This massive 3,000hp twelve-wheeler is the MLW version of the Alco Century 630, produced after MLW took over Alco's designs. The main difference is the use of MLW trucks with even wheel spacing in place of the Alco type. The

Model-Power C-628 was used as a starting point, but it is not possible to alter the bogie wheel spacing, so perhaps the purist should read no further. CN, CP and BCR all use the M-630 and the model C-628 is produced in the CN and CP colour schemes, so a little detail work can produce a passable model if the trucks are disregarded. Tyco produce a model C-630 but for Canadian use the cab end also requires modification and the method of bogie mounting makes this difficult.

The flaired rear radiators were added from 10thou styrene and one panel of the main grille at the rear of the right-hand side was filled in. 10thou styrene was also used for the dynamic brake radiator which is mounted immediately behind the cab on this type. As usual it is necessary to provide the bell and bracket, and to move the two lights down into the short hood. For the BCR model ditch lights were fitted and sun shades, horns and snow plough. Earlier versions had differently shaped radiators, and horns mounted behind the cab, while on later BCR locomotives the ditch lights were built into the low hood.

BCR operates the only M-630s fitted with the comfort cab and this particular conversion makes a most impressive model. Only the last half dozen were so fitted and BCR has recently ordered ten SD-40-2s, so presumably no more M-630 comfort cabs are likely to be built as the other railways have not ordered any further M-630s either. It is an easy job to fit the Model-Power locomotive with the comfort cab. Note that the BCR livery on this type is simplified, and without the lightning bolt stripe.

Alco C-425

This is almost indistinguishable from the C-430 which is modelled in HO by Tyco. BCR bought

Right:
A freight train on the Pacific Great Eastern (now British Columbia Railway). MLW RS-18 No 598 leads two RS-3s. Both types could be produced in HO scale from inexpensive Yugoslavian-manufactured models, while a very fine RS-3 is now available from Atlas.
Ian Allan Library

twelve of this type in 1976 from the Erie-Lackawana Railroad. Some were still operating in 1979 in EL colours with temporary BCR stickers, but ours is in line with BCR practice. Main features are the bell and horns, and the ditch lights in the low hood.

Alco/MLW RS-3

This elderly Bo-Bo type is still to be found on CP Rail and on the BCR. Our basic example, sporting the livery of BCR's predecessor, the Pacific Great Eastern, is an AHM model. The only alterations involved moving the exhaust stack and fitting the horns and bell. Other optional detail changes could involve different handrail arrangements and the provision of an old-style 'Cow-catcher' which the PGE made from steam locomotive boiler tubes! In last year's annual Chris described another conversion of this model.

MLW RS-18

The Alco RS-11 was built in Canada by MLW as the RS-11M and later the RS-18 and is similar to the less powerful RS-10. Versions with high or low short hoods are in service, and some earlier models have the long hood arranged as the front of the locomotive. Care should be taken to work from details of a specific example. The table lists the operators and the types which they own.

Operator	Manufacturer's Class	High or Low hood
VIA Rail	RS-18	H
Duluth, Winnipeg & Pacific	RS-11	H
Wabush Lake	RS-18	L
Arnaud Railway	RS-18	L
Cartier	RS-18	L
Ontario Northland	RS-10	H
British Columbia/PGE	RS-18	H&L
	RS-10	H&L
CP Rail	RS-18	H
	RS-10	H
Canadian National	RS-10	H
	RS-11M	H
	RS-18	H

The starting point for any of these is the Model-Power RS-11. The main modification to produce the MLW version is to fill and smooth up the notched corners of the hoods, providing new number boards at the same time. We used a model already finished in BCR green, but repainted the lighter green areas in a more accurate shade. Some

Below:
General Motors FP7 in CPR maroon and grey heads the westbound 'Canadian' along the Bow River at Massive, Alberta. Icicle breakers and winterisation hoods on the locomotive are clearly seen. *Canadian Pacific*

Bottom:
FP-9 No 1414, eastbound with the 'Canadian' at Banff, Alberta, retains the icicle breakers and has additional front ditch lights and rearranged handrails. *T. Pooley*

67

changes to the layout of the lights may be
necessary, while position of horns and bell seems to
be different for virtually every example.

The low hood type can be produced by cutting
away the short hood and adding a new one built up
from styrene sheet. It is necessary to provide a new
styrene cab front as well. The PGE/BCR
locomotives of this type have a large headlight
placed centrally above the windscreen, and we took
the opportunity to sleeve the bulb which is fitted
inside the model cab so that the light was directed
through the headlight.

General Motors GP-9

Chris is particularly fond of his two GP-9s, one
powered and one dummy, as they represent the kind
of luck that does not happen too often. In 1976,
nine years after Canadian Pacific changed to its new
'action red' colour scheme, he was lucky enough to
find a pair of GP-9s operating in multiple, one in the
old livery and the other in the new. The pair were
idling at Port Alberni, the end of a freight-only line
in the far west of Vancouver Island, where the
'geeps' are used in pairs as the track and the bridges
will not take heavier locomotives.

The models of Nos 8676 and 8833 are Athearn
items painted to represent the pair exactly as they
were when seen. The only modifications necessary
are the addition of a bell and bracket on the short
hood, and a triple horn. Rerailers and ditch lights
were added to No 8676, in line with current CP
practice.

Switchers

Various types of switcher (shunting locomotive)
are employed in Canada, the most common being

General Motors and Alco types. At the time of writing, the last few CP Rail Baldwin switchers are concentrated in the Vancouver area and No 7071 was chosen as the basis for adapting an Athearn Baldwin S-12 model. The main changes are the repositioning of handrails on the hood instead of the walkway, and a new exhaust stack turned up in a drill chuck from a piece of brass.

For the really discerning, the Athearn GM SW-1500 model can be adapted to produce an excellent representation of the SW-1200 version as used in Canada. A conversion kit including new truck sideframes, cab and hood modification parts, etc. is produced by Juneco and a full cab interior detail kit is available from GSB Rail.

Finally a word of comment about painting and lettering. Livery details vary so much from one locomotive to another that it is best to work from photographs of one particular machine, however an excellent general guide is available in the form of three paint diagram books *Rail Canada Vols 1-3* published by Launch Pad Distributors of Vancouver. Decals and lettering are available from several manufacturers and they differ widely in quality. The Microscale sheets seem to work very well, however the range includes only the older CP livery. The sheets are very full and detailed, with sufficient material for several items. The Walthers range has more variety, and these too are on a fairly strong base which works well. The contents of some packs are a little curious (I wish I'd known before I hand-lettered an Athearn artic truck that 'CP Transport' lettering is included in the passenger coach set!) and there is usually material for one vehicle plus some very useful left-overs. The Beaver decals which were used for the current CN

livery are on a rather brittle base which had a tendency to break up during handling. All types will, of course, need the use of a suitable decal setting agent to make them settle down neatly over details.

Although the main Canadian colours are commercially available, supplies are not always easy to obtain over here.

Budd Rail Diesel Car

This article would be incomplete without mention of the diesel railcars. Budd RDCs come in four types, varying in the amount of baggage and mail accommodation, from none in the RDC1 to full baggage and no passenger accommodation in the RDC4. Athearn produce an RDC1 and an RDC3. We have several converted to BCR condition with additional end lights and repowered with Tenshodo 'Spud' motor bogies. BCR has commenced refurbishing its small fleet and our example of this version has full fibre optic lighting.

We also have a CPR RDC3 which is a Custom Brass model made in the Far East and super-detailed to suit Canadian practice.

Below:
A General Motors SD40 of Canadian National, No 5239 is a basic model without dynamic brakes. It has extra CN fittings including ditch lights and snow hoods behind the cab. The AHM model is a good starting point for this type.
P. J. Howard

Bottom:
The Athearn SD40-2 super-detailed and finished as a typical CP Rail example in action red livery.

Right:
Another Athearn SD40-2, this time finished as BCR No 758, one of 12 examples delivered new in 1981. The model has been adapted with the Canadian Prototype Replicas 'snoot' extended small hood, which on the prototype contains slow-speed and radio control equipment.

Centre right:
A pair of VIA Rail RDC-1 railcars at Victoria, BC. Refurbishment will see many of these cars in service beyond the turn of the century. *Chris Leigh*

Bottom right:
The Athearn RDC-3 is a little short but makes a perfectly acceptable model. This example is finished as BCR No 31, extensively refurbished in 1983 and wearing the most recent colour scheme.

Modelling the North Woolwich Line

Stanley C. Jenkins, M.A.

Opened on 14 June 1847, the North Woolwich branch of the GER served the famous 'Royal Group' of docks, and there were formerly numerous sidings and connections into the docks complex. Since the War, however, the insidious growth of road transport, coupled with the gradual decline of the London docks, has robbed the railway of much of its traffic. Today, the branch traverses an area of empty basins and crumbling warehouses; one can only hope that with enlightened planning and revitalised rail links, the 'Docklands' will one day flourish once again.

Until May 1979, the western terminus of the North Woolwich service was at Tottenham Hale, on the GE Cambridge main line. On 14 May 1979, however, the re-opening of an ex-London & North Western Railway freight link between Stratford and Dalston Junction enabled the service to be diverted onto the North London Line, and the trains now terminate at Camden Road, on the LMR.

The Prototype: Description

This is one of London's most interesting, yet least known rail services. Commencing its journey at Camden Road, the DMU heads eastwards along the North London line – an interesting cross-Town link, opened in stages between 1850 and 1852. The North London is quadruple-tracked at this point, and the four tracks sweep eastwards through a heavily built-up area. The NLR stations at

Below:
Cravens two-car unit forming the 11.06 to Camden Road at North Woolwich on 29 June 1983. *Alex Dasi-Sutton*

Caledonian Road (1 mile), Highbury & Islington (1½ miles), and Canonbury (2 miles) are rather gloomy, though BR has made some attempt to brighten them up. Gaining the re-opened section east of Dalston Junction, the trains pause at the new stations at Hackney Central (3¾ miles) and Hackney Wick (5¼ miles) before finally reaching the ex-Great Eastern system at Stratford Low Level, 6¼ miles from Camden Road.

Heading southwards from the busy Stratford complex, the train begins its journey into the heart of London's docklands. Passing the site of Stratford Market station, closed in May 1957, the DMU rumbles beneath the ex-London Tilbury & Southend main line at West Ham. A new island platform here allows passenger interchange with the London Transport District Line, which runs alongside the LT&S on tracks provided by the LMS in 1932. The entrance to Canning Town station (8 miles) is now almost completely obscured by a massive flyover, and the station buildings have been rebuilt by BR. To the left, the Victorian streets of Plaistow and Canning Town survive to remind us of what the 'old time' East End of London was once like – a bustling friendly, close-knit community, with a diversity and vitality gained from intimate contact with ships and the sea.

Curving eastwards beneath the Silvertown Way, the railway enters the heart of the Royal Docks.

Passing the site of Tidal Basin station (closed following enemy action in 1943) the trains run parallel to the Royal Victoria Dock, visible over to the right; this great, man-made basin is three-quarters of a mile long, and dates from 1855.

At Custom House (Victoria Dock), 9¼ miles from Camden Road, the double track divides into two parallel single lines; all passenger trains now use the northern, or former down line, which is worked on the 'one-engine-in-steam-principle', while freight traffic uses the old up line. Custom House was once the junction for the Beckton branch, opened on 18 March 1874.

The two lines continue east for a further half mile, then turn southwards before dropping steeply into a tunnel beneath the channel separating the Royal Victoria and Royal Albert Docks. Just before the tunnel, the train passes two industrial sidings which diverge to the left. The first of these is the old Beckton branch, while the second is the PLA Gallions branch, opened on 3 August 1880 (and now lifted). These two dockland lines lost their passenger services following a major German air raid on the afternoon of Saturday 7 September 1940, when over 300 Luftwaffe bombers attacked

Below:
The 11.40 North Woolwich-Tottenham Hale, at Lea Bridge formed by a similar unit on 3 October 1977. *M. Higginson*

the East End. In the evening, a further 247 raiders dropped 335 tons of high explosive and 440 incendiary bombs into the inferno, flattening streets and blasting ships onto their sides. The docklands continued to bear the brunt of the ensuing 'Blitz', and traces of wartime damage can be discerned even today; (arguably, the East End has never recovered).

Silvertown (10¼ miles) was a small two-platform station, with GE type buildings on the former up side. Here, the parallel freight line comes to an end in a headshunt for the Silvertown Tramway, which diverges westwards to serve several riverside industrial plants. In 1978, BR and the GLC jointly rebuilt the station as a single-platform arrangement, with new, modern buildings. Heading east once more, the branch runs parallel to the Royal Albert and the King George V Docks, though the traveller can see very little, as long rows of terraced houses flank the northern side of the line. To the right, the Silvertown headshunt finally ends at a buffer stop, and the North Woolwich branch train enters its terminus on a solitary single line.

North Woolwich once boasted a relatively lavish terminal station, but severe rationalisation, which followed the introduction of DMUs in the 1960s,

reduced the terminus to a basic single track, and BR has now provided a new station amid the ruins of the old. An unusual feature of the old station was its turntable – sited in front of the classical style station buildings. This unorthodox feature was removed about 55 years ago, but the circular 'well' in the platforms survived thereafter to puzzle the uninitiated traveller! Also of interest were the curious 'S' shaped platforms, which were presumably a relic of the days when the four terminal roads converged towards the turntable.

The Plan

For the modeller, the North Woolwich line provides an interesting urban branch, with plenty of scope for freight operation. The plan shown is an attempt to extract certain salient features of the branch and compress them onto a 14ft × 9ft baseboard. These features include the unique terminal arrangements at North Woolwich, the dock lines, lineside industries, and two of the intermediate stations. It is envisaged that the layout would be primarily steam-worked, and this would mean a pre-1961/62 historical setting (unless one adopts a 'flexible' period, say 1960-1970). Ideally, the scheme would best suit an LNER modeller, who could build up a stud of small and medium-sized

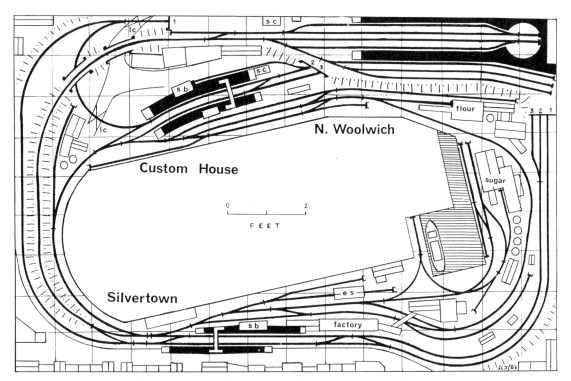

locomotives, such as 'N7' 0-6-2Ts, 'L1' 2-6-4Ts, 'F6' 2-4-2Ts, 'J15' 0-6-0s and 'B1' 4-6-0s.

The model train services would start and terminate at North Woolwich, where five long passenger roads provide ample storage space; there are in addition two multi-purpose goods roads, though no attempt has been made to recreate the prototype goods facilities. From the terminus, trains descend a long gradient to join the continuous run, which provides either conventional double track running or two independent single track main lines. Supposing that the latter option is to be followed, our train will take the outer circuit and run through Silvertown non-stop. Passing beneath North Woolwich, the train then makes one full trip round the outer line before pulling into the inner platform at Silvertown. This little station is depicted fairly accurately, with short, staggered platforms linked by a footbridge and flanked by Victorian terraced houses and shops. Although there are no goods facilities as such, a connecting line diverges behind the station to serve the Port of London Authority system, of which more anon.

Running now on the inner circuit, trains leave Silvertown and re-enter the tunnel beneath North Woolwich, emerging at Custom House. Spacious, up and down platforms are provided here and, as at

Silvertown, there is a link to the PLA lines; a glance at the plan will show that this station is situated on a passing loop, which continues into the tunnel to provide hidden storage facilities. Leaving Custom House, trains can make further trips round the inner main line, or else turn sharp right in order to gain the return loop; having taken the loop, up workings automatically become down trains, ready to retrace their path back to North Woolwich.

PLA Lines

Although the BR part of the layout is almost entirely passenger-orientated, an extensive industrial system serves several docks, warehouses and factories. The PLA lines form a 'layout within a layout', and consist of a lengthy main line, two marshalling areas, a small motive power depot, and sidings to various lineside installations. In reality, these included chemical works, sugar refineries, scrap yards, a glass works, gas works, and many other industries. Several industries are suggested on the plan, giving scope for the 'playing card' system of operation, in which each wagon number is noted on a small card which is dealt at the start of each session. Having deposited each card in boxes representing individual destinations (such as the 'sugar refinery', the 'flour mill' and the 'jetty') one

then has to shunt each vehicle to its allotted place, giving rise to a realistic simulation of full size operation!

Scenic potential is vast; an easy option would be to make use of the familiar Bilteezi building sheets – particularly the 'Factory Sheet' which represents the sort of 20th century steel-framed industrial buildings found around the London Docks (unfortunately, most London buildings are made of yellow-grey bricks, whereas the Bilteezi kit is a red brick, Midlands style structure). The sharp curves in the dock area could use up commercial 'train set' sharp curves – the dock lines would be sunk into wharves like tram lines. Ships present a problem in terms of sheer size; a small, modern vessel such as a 9,100 ton 'SD14' cargo ship would be as long as a six-coach train if modelled to anything like scale size! In view of this it is perhaps best to depict the large ships on painted back-drops, and model smaller craft such as tugs, sailing barges, and narrow boats (narrow boats were sometimes towed downstream to the Royal Docks – a hazardous voyage for such small vessels).

The PLA abandoned steam power in July 1961, but as this is a historical layout there would be scope for a quite large fleet of 0-4-0 and 0-6-0 industrial tanks. Typical builders would have been

Above:
Silvertown station on 7 August 1984 with the Tate & Lyle sugar factory and the former Silvertown Tramway diverging to the right. *S. C. South*

Hunslet, Fowler and Hudswell Clarke. (Freelance modellers could utilize ready to run models such as those by Hornby. Scratch-builders might have fun producing one or two self-propelled steam cranes – which are, as a matter of interest, some of the few surviving private 'locomotives' in modern dock yards, which have in general abandoned railway operation.

This article describes the North Woolwich line as it was until May 1985. From that date the electrified Richmond-Broad St service was extended from Dalston Junction to North Woolwich, with the line being electrified on the third rail system. Thereafter trains have been formed of Southern Region Class 416 2-EPB electric multiple units, which have replaced the DMU sets previously used to North Woolwich and the Class 501 EMUs on the North London line from Richmond.

Below:
Abbey Lane, Stratford, on the same date, with a Class 105 unit passing on a North Woolwich-Camden Road service. *S. C. South*

Dawn's Promising Light

Peter Jones

**Introducing the Compton Down
Railway**

It is one of those brilliant early mornings in spring. There is still just a touch of frost in the shadows and not a breath of wind is felt. It is just the right time to be out in the garden. Model railways out of doors are just as much about the changing seasons and moods as about the last rivet. The tiny wheel clicks mingle with the subdued chatter of a diesel loco or the panting of a steam engine working hard against a gradient. There are also the smells – like damp grass, creosote and warm oil punctuated by the nostalgic astringency of burning meths. There are trains to be run and there is real pleasure to be enjoyed.

The Compton Down Railway has been slowly growing over the years and still the work goes on. The long term aim is towards a fully integrated narrow gauge slate railway in 16mm:1ft scale, with the emphasis on providing a true to life setting in which to run the trains. Thus progress tends to be along the lines of large earthworks and sculpture. In particular, constructive use of height is incorporated. Indeed, there are many new ideas being incorporated to take the concept on from the plain 'flat track round the shrubbery' (delightful though this particular hobby is) towards something more ambitious. Actually, to claim ideas as new is rather a presumption – rather it is drawing together the threads of many ideas – some going back to the last century.

It is intended in due course to present a series of occasional articles to describe some of these ideas, but for now the two illustrations may give some idea of what the basis of these will be.

Below:
A Hudson Hunslet clatters along gallery No 2 of Llanbedr quarry with assorted slate wagons in tow. The early morning shadows are still sharp and clear.

Below:
At the same time a Decauville tank collects oddments from the end of gallery No 3 and trundles down the bank. The 'trees' in the background are a box hedge trimmed to look the part.

The Meadowdale Light Railway Co.

D. H. Thompson

Photographs by M. Jackson

Meadowdale is a small country town situated in the North Yorkshire moors about six miles from the sea. It is served by a single line branch railway running to join the main line to the large industrial complex in the north and via a junction to a large market town to the south. There appears to be no reason for the town's existence except for a small shopping centre and market for the surrounding farms and estates. That is until about 1890, when a seam of coal was found high up in the hillside quite near the railway but not near enough to be able to install a siding allowing the mined coal to be dropped into the wagons by chute. Two astute local

shop-keepers, Walter Hackit and Henry Loader decided as local benefactors that some of the local unemployed required something to use up their surplus energy and set them to work digging out the seam. Pack horses were used at first to carry the coal in baskets down the bankside to Meadowdale station yard for local sale, any surplus being sent by rail to the north. Both these business gentlemen made a steady profit over the following twenty years improving the output and conditions to such

Below:
A general view with the mine building at the front and High Moor station and village above.

78

Above:
The mine building with a narrow gauge train headed by a Peco tank passing in front.

an extent that thirty men were employed by 1910. Then a retired mill owner from West Yorkshire decided to settle for his retirement in the little village of High Moor overlooking Meadowdale.

Sir Jasper Black, 70 years, who came to be known as 'Jasper the Grasper' because of his meanness soon tired of inactivity and decided to use some of his fortune in developing local industry. He bought the mine from the two local gentlemen, at what appeared to be a reasonable sum, enabling them to retire into comfortable old age. Sir Jasper decided that clean graded coal would realise bigger profits and installed the mine building with modern cleaning equipment. Then he improved transport arrangements by building a narrow gauge railway with horse drawn wagons to run from the mine building to the station yard and brickworks. Later two small 0-4-0 engines, Nos 1 and 2 were employed. The output of the mine soared as did the profits but wages and conditions remained the same. Soon this exploitation resulted in the seam becoming nearly worked out and the miners going on extended strike. The mine and buildings fell into disrepair and were closed down. Sir Jasper, now 81 realised that some of his money was being wasted took a gamble on what he hoped would be a good investment and also a public amenity. He built a

small station behind the town station and commenced a narrow gauge railway to connect many of the small villages over the hill in Martindale, the fishing villages on the coast, and later a return line up the Valley of Trees.

The construction of the line took some five years due to the necessity of providing a number of tunnels and viaducts and as each village was reached, a passenger service to Meadowdale was commenced. Owing to the high cost of track-laying the locomotives and rolling stock were a motley collection of secondhand vehicles for ths most part and only occasionally was any new stock introduced. Sir Jasper died at the ripe old age of 93 when the line was just beginning to show a reasonable return and declared on his deathbed that free transport would be provided for all local inhabitants for one week in the year. Engines Nos 1 and 2 were used to assist in the construction and are still running.

The layout is modelled as in the early 1930s, showing Meadowdale Station and goods yard with the narrow gauge station engine shed, coaling stage and unloading siding behind. The dilapidated coal mine building is to the left (re-opened following the discovery of iron ore) above which you can see the village of High Moor. To the right of the village and behind the mine building is a small water wheel used to generate electricity for the mine buildings and Meadowdale town (another of Sir Jasper's enterprises). On the right is the brickworks with the scout camp in the corner (front). The baseboards number four, the centre two are 6ft × 2ft the outer two being 4ft × 3ft fastened together with coach bolts. The baseboards are constructed from 2in × 1in wood braced at 1ft intervals. The scenery is built up with expanded polystyrene covered with mutton cloth and later a little Polyfilla is added before painting. The rock faces are cork bark and in some places any tree bark that can be found. Much of the scenery is finished off with flock powder or dyed sawdust. The buildings are nearly all proprietary products in either plastic or printed card.

The track is Peco 'Crazy Track' and the points mainly Marcway (live frog type) are laid on cork-covered felt to simulate ballast. Most of the points are electrically operated but some of the concealed ones are manually operated via point levers. The controllers are two Scalespeed P16+ transistorised units, output being 12V dc. Supply to controllers is from a Scalespeed Transformer with two 16-18V ac outputs. The controller allows simulated slow starting and stopping.

The locomotives are products of Playcraft, Minitrains, Eggerbahn and Liliput plus Gem and Peco cast white metal bodies on Arnold Chassis. The Board of Directors may decide on the purchase or building of further motive power (finances allowing) and also allowing running powers to foreign locomotives for testing purposes. Some of the rolling stock is from the same manufacturers with others from Mikes Models, Ian Kirk and Festiniog. Some of the locomotives and stock have been slightly modified. The standard colours are blue for locomotives, blue and cream for coaches and anything goes for freight vehicles.

Standard gauge track is Peco Streamline at present laid on foam underlay, all visible points being electrically operated. The rolling stock is somewhat varied and normally consists of converted Triang Clerestory coaches in NER or LNER livery or private owner wagons either kit or hand built. Some of the locomotives available from the owners stock are not really suitable for the depicted period but it is hoped that this will be remedied shortly. The control equipment is identical to that of the narrow gauge.

Above:
Another view of the mine building, with the forge beyond.

Above:
Narrow gauge train returns from the Valley of the Trees. Note hikers and shepherd.

Below:
The LNER 'G5' tank stands outside Meadowdale shed.

Below:
0-4-0ST *Prince* passing the forge.

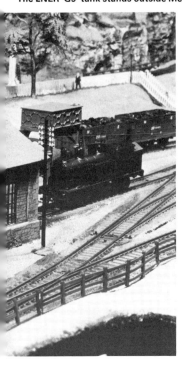

Wills LNER 'K3' Kit

S. J. Barnfield

The 'K3' 2-6-0s were a development by Gresley of his earlier 'K1' and 'K2' classes, and the first 10 were built by the Great Northern Railway in 1920. As such they had the GNR type of cab with no side windows, and GNR tender. The LNER built more of them after Grouping in 1924/25 and these were built at Darlington and appeared with the NER-type cab with two side windows, and the first type of LNER group standard tender, with stepped out sides. The first 10 built by the GNR were also given this type of tender at about that time.

The prototype represented by the Wills kit is the version built from approximately 1928 on, when the second type of group standard tender with flush sides was first introduced. Unfortunately no one manufactures a kit for the first of the LNER group standard tenders although the early GNR type is available. Therefore unless one is willing to scratchbuild a tender it is not possible to construct a model of the early LNER K3s.

I have been unable to obtain photographic evidence of a GNR-built 'K3' in LNER days just prior to World War 2 with a GNR type tender. I would be grateful to anyone who could provide this. However, the kit as built does represent quite a high proportion of the prototypes and there must be hundreds of photographs available showing these.

The kit itself is one of the fairly early ones produced by Wills and was designed to take the Triang 2-6-2 chassis. This has not been available for quite some time and although I have one spare I wanted to make the locomotive available for both the club layout, which is fine scale 00 and my own which is EM. Fortunately I also had a spare tender available so all I had to do was build two separate chassis. As the Wills kit is designed to take the Triang chassis the locomotive body is a scale 6in too short, so therefore the coupled wheelbase had to be shortened by that amount and instead of being 7ft 6in and 8ft 9in I made it 7ft 3in and 8ft 6in.

So that the two chassis were exactly the same, I soldered together 4 pieces of 1/16in thick strip brass. Using the Skinley drawing, these were cut to 127mm long by 20mm wide. I then marked out the

LNER 'K3' class 2-6-0 No 159 at Doncaster. *T. G. Hepburn*

Above:
The two chassis assemblies for the author's 'K3'.

relative positions of the axle holes and drilled these out in a pillar drill, making sure that everything was flat and square. The shape of the mainframe was then scribed onto the brass and cut out with a piercing saw, finishing off with fine Swiss needle files to the correct shape.

Up to that point I had not decided what type of motor to use in these chassis, and I found that if an XO4 or MW005 type was to be used this would project backwards into the cab. However, after making enquiries in my local model shop I decided to use an Anchoridge Japanese motor. The two types that would fit easily were the D11 and D13. I thought the D11 a little too small for the kit, so the D13 it was. The mainframes were marked out to receive this and duly cut out. These were then split and soldered up in the normal way, using Eames frame jigs to keep everything square. Four coupling rods were cut from rail, and wheels etc fitted to the chassis.

For the EM chassis I decided to use the superb wheels manufactured by Mike Sharman. The axles were cut to length and fitted on three of the wheels. As the motor ran fairly fast, Mike's 50-1 gears were used and the gear was fitted on the centre axle and the other three wheels pushed on, and quartered. I was very satisfied to find that the chassis sat flat and square with no wobble. It is very easy to allow a few thou to creep in here and there to spoil things.

For the 00 chassis 21mm Romford wheels were used, and although 1mm undersize, the overscale flanges tend to disguise this. Again Mike's 50-1 gears were used, and I found that after the body had been weighted they gave good hauling capacity and very slow running. Eames LNER valve gear was used on both chassis together with their LNER cylinder assemblies. A Kemilway etched brass kit was used for the brake gear, and since this has been on the market, has made life very easy for those wishing to detail chassis.

Below:
The author's completed Wills kit as No 1117.

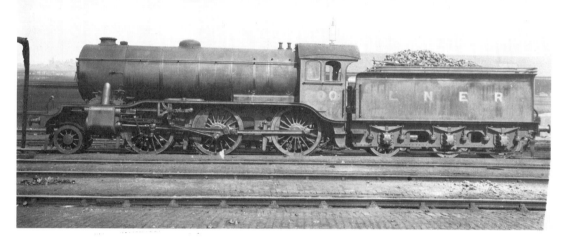

As I said earlier the body kit is an early one made by Wills and is quite basic compared with their later ones. Two important modifications have to be made to the kit. Firstly, providing the ventilator for the cab roof and secondly, removing the hump over the front buffer beam, where provision is made for fitting the Triang chassis. Not only is this unsightly but it is very unprototypical.

Apart from these modifications, provision had to be made for fitting the chassis to the body, and to do this, I soldered two pieces of brass to the body. One at the rear behind the cab footsteps, and the other underneath the body, just behind the smokebox saddle. This was drilled 8BA clearance and an 8BA

Above:
A broadside view of 'K3' No 200. *LPC/Ian Allan Library*

nut was soldered on top, to match a spacer already in place in the chassis, and the rear one slotted to accept a piece of brass projecting from the rear of the chassis.

After final cleaning up and filling any gaps eg that along the top of the boiler, the locomotive was finished in Floquil paints, and lettered and numbered with Methfix transfers.

Below:
No 1117 in EM guise heads a typical freight train.

Hand-operated Level Crossing Gates

Eric W. J. Walford

What goes on below the baseboards is often infinitely more interesting than the action above, for it is here that 'magic' is performed to bring looks of amazement to the onlookers, as many can testify from past exhibition experience. Judging by the comments, one can be forgiven for believing that we are a bunch of geniuses whose below-board mechanics are so utterly complicated that everything above is made to work, often perfectly, though more often, not so perfectly.

With the many exhibitions I have been to both as an exhibitor and a visitor, the one thing which has always stuck in my mind is the lack of level crossings one sees on layouts, and of those which do exist, I have yet to see gates which actually work, as opposed to being rigidly glued down to the baseboard. Here then is one answer to the problem of how to make those gates work.

The principle of my method uses gears, wheels and moving gate posts. If this method has already been thought of, then I haven't seen it and it is coincidental.

Fig 1 shows the mechanics for a single line crossing, showing only one mechanism, two being required – one for each of the gates.

The idea is to turn handle (**K**) thereby rotating the crown wheel (**F**) via the driving rod (**G**), transmitted through crown wheel (**E**) and up through the turned brass post (**D**) which is part of the gate post (**A**), finally turning the gates (**L**).

The parts in which tolerances are critical are: brass bush (**C**); and supporting plate (**H**), plus the moving gate post spindle (**D**).

No dimensions will be given because this method can be used with equal effect on any scale from 2mm upwards.

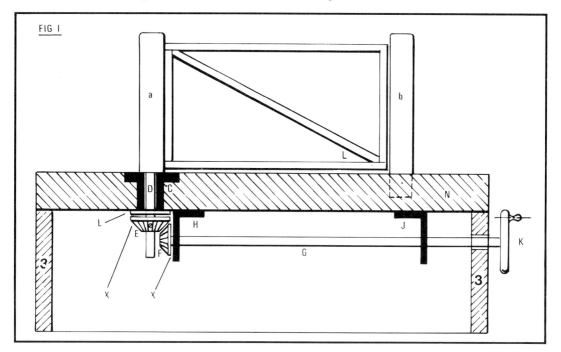

FIG I

Brass Bush (C). This part is turned and reamed out in the normal way, that is to say, face, turn, and bore, followed by reaming of the bore. Whatever dimensions are chosen, ensure that a fair thickness of metal remains in the proximity of the bore, say a minimum of ⅛in. The bore must be nice and smooth in finish and the piece must be precision-turned to close tolerances as far as the bore is concerned. **Fig 2** gives a close-up of the item, with dimensions suitable for 3mm and 4mm scale. Note that the boss does not have to be too large, but just enough to prevent it from falling through the baseboard when sunk in position.

Gate Post (A). This can be made from square brass rod of a size suitable for the scale for which it is required. **Fig 3** shows the part. Note that the lower portion is turned, (a good finish is required with no feed marks), and is flat on one side for the lower part of the item. This area will accommodate the grub screw of the crown wheel to which it will later be attached. I suggest that sufficient metal is

removed from the round portion to ensure that there is sufficient 'flat' at the base of the squared portion to enable the post to rest on the face surface of the boss of the bush (C). File away the corners very gently, just sufficient to prevent jagged edges from scoring the surface of the bush. So little metal needs to be removed that it is hardly noticeable.

Support Plates (H) and (J). Fig 4 shows the finished plates. I have shown two in **Fig 1**, but more can be added if the distance warrants it. The important plate is (H) nearest the crown wheel (F), (see **Fig 1**). This plate is used to prevent the horizontal play along driving rod (G). If there is too much play, the crown wheels will not mesh properly, thus spoiling the operation of the gates, so the closer plate (H) can be got to the back of crown wheel (F), the better. Plate (J) is only for horizontal support and general guidance, but even so, when fitted, both plates must be in total alignment with each other. When drilling holes in the plates, allow a tolerance of no more than 2thou (1thou on the cross-slide marker), in relation to the outside diameter of the driving rod (G). I reamed out the holes in the support plates to ensure a smooth finish, not relying on drilling, however keen the tool. Note that the plates are angled 90deg on one edge, in which are drilled two holes each and then counter-sunk. The plates *must* be screwed securely to the underside of the baseboard to prevent any movement at all.

Drive Rod (G). I made mine from normal ¼in brass rod, turned down to 3/16in along its length, minus 2thou in relation to the plates (H) and (J). Before turning the rod, determine the length

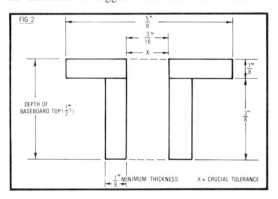

FIG 2

DEPTH OF BASEBOARD TOP (½")

⅛" MINIMUM THICKNESS   X = CRUCIAL TOLERANCE

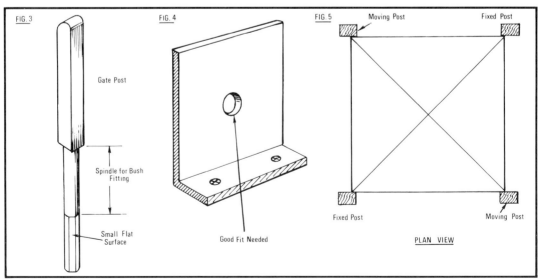

FIG. 3

Gate Post

Spindle for Bush Fitting

Small Flat Surface

FIG. 4

Good Fit Needed

FIG. 5   Moving Post   Fixed Post

Fixed Post   Moving Post

PLAN VIEW

required. This must be sufficient to cover the distance through the baseboard edge batten and up to the point where the vertical gate post and crown-wheel are to be sited. Allow a little surplus to be sure as this can be removed later if need be. At this stage the cranking wheel (K) can be made to ones own wishes. Mine was turned from an off-cut of 1in brass rod, suitably bored out to provide a push-fit onto the drive rod (G), which I then stuck firmly with epoxy adhesive.

Crown Wheels (E) and (F). These should be on the small side, not more than an outside diameter of ½in. It is best to buy these, (four are required for a two-gate set-up), in which case the drive rod (G) and gate post spindle (D) must be machined to suit the bore of the manufactured parts. Be sure the wheels are fitted with grub screws.

Miscellaneous. The only items left to make are the gates themselves and the posts (B), both of which are simple enough to make from wood.

Assembly. The first thing to do is to mark out the site on the baseboard edge accurately. **Fig 5** shows the area, and note that the four posts are equi-distant to each other since it is a single track set-up. The posts are set diagonally so that the revolving posts are opposite each other, likewise the fixed posts which the drawing clearly indicates. Having marked out, first drill out the baseboard surface ready to house one of the brass bushes (C). Measure off, using the gate itself, and drill out the corresponding fixed post hole. Repeat the process for the other gate ensuring that all distances are equal. Now sink the bushes into place ensuring that the surfaces of the bosses are flush with the surface

of the baseboard. These can now be glued home or, if the hole is tight enough, a push fit will do the same job. I never rely on this as being sufficient to keep the bushes in place over a long period, especially with regular use of the gates, so they are stuck down as well.

Next, drop the moving posts (A) one into each bush and check that they rotate freely but without too much play in the vertical. If the bush holes and post spindles have been turned correctly this should be a routine check and nothing more. If not, then another post or bush will have to be turned although this check should be done when the parts are made. Assuming all parts to be correct, now slip washer (L) onto the spindle from below the board followed by one of the crown wheels. Fit it so that there is as little play as possible in the vertical position of the post/spindle, and secure the grub screw gently but firmly so that the screw bites the flat portion of the spindle.

The next job is to take the drive rod with its attached crank wheel or handle, (K) and line it up the end with crown wheel. Having ensured that the drive rod is in line with the wheel, drill out the baseboard batten, having also checked that this hole is at the same height below the baseboard to correspond with those in the supporting plates (H) and (J). A reasonable-sized hole should be drilled to allow for adjustment of the drive shaft later on, since it is not crucial but simply to allow access of

Below:
All the paraphernalia of a pure Great Western level crossing at Hartlebury, junction for the Severn Valley line as seen on 19 September 1959. *V. R. Webster*

the rod through the batten. Now push the drive rod through the batten and slide both supporting plates onto the shaft followed by the crown wheel (F) which should not be fixed at this stage. Line up the shaft ensuring that both crown wheels mesh in their centres and carefully secure supporting plate (J) to the underside of the baseboard. Slide plate (H) along the drive rod and having ensured that the crown wheel (F) meshes correctly, secure the wheel, having first removed any surplus material from the end of the drive rod. Now, bring up supporting plate (H) and holding it firmly, as close behind Crown wheel (F) as possible to prevent horizontal play, secure the plate in the same manner as plate (J). There should now be no play either in the revolving post (A) or in the actual drive rod. If this is not so, adjust as conditions dictate, the idea being that the crowns will not lose their mesh. The process is repeated for the other gate and the final

job is to fix the fixed posts into their positions, and check that when the gates open and close, that they meet their respective posts in both the open and closed positions. Paint the posts and gates and when dry, oil all moving parts of the mechanisms and you have yourself a set of operating crossing-gates.

Just one last item. If crown wheels are not forthcoming, bevel gears can be used in lieu. Bonds have them, coming in ratios of 1:1, 2:1, 3:1 and 4:1. If used, adjustment will be needed to the height of the holes drilled in supporting plates (H) and (J). Bore sizes range as follows:

1:1 and 2:1 – ⅛in-½in
3:1 – ³⁄₁₆in only
4:1 – ¼in only.

Below:
A standard Southern Railway gated level crossing at Betchworth. *Ian Allan Library*

Above:
'J36' No 65267 at Bathgate level crossing with train for Bathgate Lower. *M. Pope*

Below:
Gated SR level crossing at Battle as seen in 1969. *J. Scrace*

Thinking about Operation

John Hughes

One of the most attractive features of the hobby of railway modelling is the extent to which it comprises a whole range of different sub-hobbies, all uniting to produce the finished effect. Photography, metal-working, electronics, painting and drawing, and a host of other interests all have their part to play, and one of the great benefits of club membership is that it enables one to meet with fellow modellers who may possess the skills that we ourselves lack.

That said, however, there is one aspect of modelling which has received far less than its share of attention, especially on this side of the Atlantic. I refer to operation. Indeed, to a large number of modellers, the very term is almost meaningless; operation, to them, is what you do when you have finished constructing a model, and involves either running it round and round in circles, or, in a more 'prototypical' manner, from terminus to fiddle yard and back.

That is not to say, of course, that there have not been some superlative models built primarily with operation in mind, one of the most popular and successful being the well-known Yatton Junction, with its well-ordered procession of main- and branch-line trains. But, for the most part, many people seem content to operate in only the most rudimentary manner, doing a little random shunting in between the arrival and departure of trains, but little else. Others, perhaps with an eye to being more true to the prototype, actually operate to something approaching a prototype timetable; but even there, there is often a good deal of room for improvement.

Let me make it plain at the outset that I am in no way attacking any of these ways of running a layout; if that's what you want to do, then it's your good right to go ahead and do it – I think it says so somewhere in Magna Carta. As with so much else in this hobby, what works best for you may not work for me, and vice versa. But if you are feeling a little bored by the set-up you have at the moment, then a little more sophisticated operation may be the very thing that you need to reawaken your interest.

Let us start with the simple business of designing the main station of the traditional fiddle yard scheme. The best place to begin is to try and decide how much running you expect to be able to carry out in a typical operating 'day' of, say, about three hours. If you decide that you can handle three full-length goods trains in addition to the passenger traffic, and the run-round loop will accommodate a dozen vehicles or so, then your station plan *must* be able to accommodate the arrival (and departure) of 36 vehicles a session. Since the real railways don't generally expect to pick up in the afternoon the same vehicles that they dropped off that morning (there are some notable exceptions, but we can forget these for the moment) our terminal must therefore be able to accommodate at least the same number of vehicles as our daily arrivals total, assuming that all the stuff that came in 'yesterday' will in fact be leaving 'today'. Actually, it is better to assume that some vehicles will have a rather longer turnaround (especially coal trucks) and since we don't want the goods yard to be choked the whole time, we should allow at least half as much space again as we would need to turn everything around in a 'day'. For our notional 36 trucks a day, that means a goods yard capable of handling about 54 vehicles simultaneously, ie with about 14 feet of clear siding space. If that doesn't seem a lot, then go back through some published plans and add up the total siding allocations in some of the branch-line stations; better still, go upstairs and measure how much space you have.

If your layout is already built, and you can't increase the siding space at all, then all is not lost. For the most enjoyable operation you will be restricted in any one operating 'day' to bringing in and taking out trains equal to not more than about two-thirds of the total capacity of the sidings. This figure can be increased by using a higher proportion of stock of the quick turnaround variety (e.g. horse-boxes, milk tanks and the like); or you can compromise by running mixed trains, which will both cut down the total number of goods vehicles you can bring in, and will give you some interesting shunting problems as you dodge the coach which is sitting in the platform road.

As regards the *kind* of traffic that will be operated over your line, the more variety that is possible (within reasonable limits) the better. Most small branch termini survived on a fairly dull diet of inward coal and farm equipment, including fertiliser and machinery, and outward agricultural traffic supplemented by any local raw materials from quarries and the like. If that seems like sufficient variety for you, then fine. Of course, if you're following a prototype situation, then the decision as to what sort of traffic you can have will have been taken from you in any case. But there are a few dodges that can be used to add a little more variety. One of the best is a wharf. If one assumes that the goods are going on a further journey by boat, then almost anything can be logically carried. Some industries, too, demand a wider range of stock than others. A furniture factory, for example, will need inbound timber, foam, upholstery, coal (for the boilers), and perhaps empty packing cases, while providing outbound traffic in crates. A quarry, on the other hand, will have only the occasional inward carriage of machinery to offset the regular exchange of explosives in, stone out.

Assuming that the station is capable of storing the stock, how efficiently can it handle it? Of course, every prototype railway had the occasional station that was next to impossible to shunt properly, but this happened either because of the topography of the area, or because the traffic at a station grew and the land was not available to expand. In any case, many prototype stations that seem on a plan to have been difficult to shunt were actually handled either by horses or by capstans that pulled the wagons along, a solution that is not available to us small-scale modellers! Therefore, avoid any temptation to create a shunting puzzle. One road that must be shunted from the opposite direction to the others will provide quite enough difficulty for most purposes. (If you can't altogether keep clear of puzzles, then you can always set one up by declaring, for example, that the length of the headshunt has been reduced because one end of it is occupied by S&T vehicles. Another possible operational 'difficulty' that can be set up when the

whim strikes is to forbid locomotives to travel past a certain point on a siding, on the excuse that the rail is damaged, so that all stock has to be placed or retrieved by means of a 'reach train' of empty vehicles.)

One planning trick that is frequently beneficial is to allow the sidings to fall away from the headshunt on a slight gradient. The effects of this are two-fold: in the first place, totally flat yard areas were generally avoided on the prototype, since they were difficult to drain, so that a slight difference in levels improves the appearance of the station. Secondly, the slight falling gradient will make it much easier for trains to be backed into the sidings without mishap, and problems such as buffer locking and wheels 'picking' at points will be much reduced. Conversely, the tension on the couplings when pulling a train out of the sidings will make accidental uncoupling impossible. But the gradient should not be so severe that the shunter is prone to slip – something of the order of one in a hundred is probably a good figure to aim at; and of course changes in gradient should not take place too close to points.

How long should the headshunt be? My rule of thumb here is that it should be no shorter than one and a half times the length of the longest siding that feeds off it; some prototype headshunts were a great deal shorter than that, especially where they fed into little-used sidings, but the majority were far longer. Not all prototype stations had headshunts. Lyme Regis, for example, lacked one, as did many small passing stations on lightly-used single track lines.

A worthwhile way of improving the shunting opportunities at a small terminus is to assign more than one function to each of the roads, so that, for example, the track that services the goods shed might also serve the end-loading ramp. If an industry is placed on a siding, it might have more than one loading door, so that the shunting crew must put incoming vehicles in the correct place; this may well entail the removal of any blocking vehicles so that the delivery can be carried out.

Implicit in all this is the fact that the goods yard does not serve merely as a place in which the stock is to be stored in between movements in trains; rather it should provide a place in which the vehicles can be loaded or unloaded as efficiently as possible, so that they can be directed to some other revenue-earning task. In other words, each siding should be conceived with some useful activity in mind.

Southern Steam to Padstow

Peter Kazmierczak

It's a long way from London to Padstow in Cornwall. In the 1950s and early 1960s you could catch the 11.11 'Atlantic Coast Express' out of Waterloo and be in Padstow in time for tea at 17.20. Today you have to make tracks for Paddington to catch the 11.25 'Cornish Riviera' and after changing at Bodmin Road (now renamed Bodmin Parkway), arrive at Padstow by Western National bus at 17.05. Whilst the journey today is doubtless more comfortable, it is far less interesting overall. This contrasts with the ride behind steam over Southern metals where apart from the changing scenery from the bustle of London to the peace and open spaces of the West Country, the journey itself was more varied.

After the complexities of Waterloo and Clapham Junction, the train would be getting into its stride by Berrylands. On through the commuter belt past Woking and out of the electrified area; dashing through Fleet and Winchfield, past Basingstoke and under the Bournemouth line at Battledown. Now on the West of England line, speed would rise into the 90s as we tore through Andover Junction and headed for our first stop at Salisbury. Here the first portion of the train was detached, this would follow us as an all-stations local to Exeter. Along the Dorset/Somerset border speed would again reach the 90 mark whilst Devon might greet us with the magic 100mph at Axminster. Following the climb to Honiton Tunnel would be our next stop at Sidmouth Junction, the through carriages for Sidmouth and Exmouth being detached. Shortly, the large locomotive depot on our right marked the approach to Exeter, where the train divided. The front part went off first to Ilfracombe with a portion for Torrington. We sat tight for a further 10 minutes until we made for Okehampton where we lost the Plymouth portion, and thence to Halwill Junction where the Bude carriage was removed. Only 50 miles to go but still 1¾ hours of travelling time left as we now call at all stations. Tower Hill has a very metropolitan-sounding name and for a moment we

think we are back in London. However, calling at Tresmeer, Camelford and Delabole makes us realise that we are indeed in Cornwall. Only a few stops now to Padstow and journey's end.

This line to Padstow was one of the three main routes of the London and South Western Railway. At Grouping the ex-LSWR lines became the Western Section of the Southern Railway and later, with Nationalisation, eventually became the South Western Division of British Railways Southern Region. Today most of the ex-LSWR lines west of Exeter have gone and those that remain are part of the Western Region. Indeed, with Laira-based Class 50s and WR rolling stock working the Waterloo to Exeter service it's now a case of 'Great' Western rules OK!

Both the other main SR routes are still with us although for the most part now electrified. The first to Portsmouth received its third rail electric current before World War 2. This line leaves the others at Woking and after passing Guildford climbs up over the South Downs before falling to sea level at Portsmouth. The other main line, to Bournemouth and beyond, parts company with the West of England route just past Basingstoke. After dropping through Winchester and Eastleigh to Southampton, it then meanders through the New Forest to Bournemouth. The electrification carried out in 1967 ends here but trains continue behind diesel power to Dorchester and finally (over ex-Great Western metals) into Weymouth.

These ex-LSWR lines are extremely popular with modellers. Most of the branch termini such as Swanage, Lyme Regis, Seaton, Sidmouth and Bude have been recreated in miniature and have appeared in the model railway journals. Through stations based on Halwill Junction, Crewkerne and the South Dorset area have also been built. Also there have been many layouts based on fictitious lines in the region, the most famous being Charford which has given me (and I imagine many other people too) a lot of inspiration in their modelling.

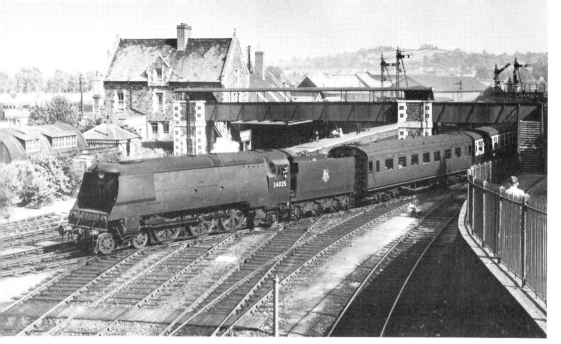

Above:
Typifying the SR in Devon, 'West Country' Pacific No 34025
***Whimple* takes the Ilfracombe branch at Barnstaple**
Junction on 11 August 1955. *R. E. Vincent*

Now what makes one layout more successful or more effective than another? The usual answer is atmosphere; it is easy to say but how do we achieve this? One way is by the types of locomotives we run on the layout. For example a model of part of the East Coast main line set in the 1950s just wouldn't look right without Gresley's 'A4' Pacifics. The Western Region line through Devon in the 1960s wouldn't be the same without some 'Warships' whilst a layout based on the West Coast main line in the 1970s, no matter how well constructed and detailed, would have to have some Class 86 electrics bouncing around on it. But it is more than the actual types operating on the layout, it is the balance of types typical of an area which is important. Let me illustrate this by looking at the distribution of ex-Southern steam locomotives on the Western Section of the SR. The chosen date (August 1950) was selected for the following reason: There was a wide variety of locomotive classes operating in the area at a time when the popular Bulleid Pacifics were in service but before the introduction of BR standard classes, which led to a reduction in variety due to the withdrawal of older types. Information about specific locomotive numbers is available to all in the form of *1950 Locoshed Book* which was reprinted by Ian Allan in 1973.

Now, in considering which classes of locomotive are typical of an area we need to look beyond the allocation of the local shed. For example, engines working in the Barnstaple area of North Devon, as well as coming from the local shed would also come from Exmouth Junction and to a lesser extent from sheds further east such as Salisbury. Hence, we first need to look at the Western Section as a whole. The map shows the location of locomotive depots on the Southern from Nine Elms in London to Wadebridge in the far west. I have excluded the Isle of Wight as obviously its locomotives were confined to the island. The Somerset and Dorseh line is also excluded as its motive power was loaned from the London Midland Region and specific to that line. Finally, the Southern shed at Reading is left out as, although coming under Nine Elms wing, it was a former South Eastern and Chatham depot and its allocation and workings were generally on the Central and Eastern Sections of the Region.

We are left with 16 depots whose allocations account for about 45% of Southern stock. The different classes and the number at each of these sheds is shown on the accompanying diagram; for example the 'MN' (Merchant Navy) class was allocated to three sheds on the section at Nine Elms, Salisbury and Exmouth Junction whilst the 'USA' tanks were concentrated at one depot – Southampton.

Although at first sight this diagram looks rather forbidding it does show the distribution of the various classes through the area. Types like the 'T9' 4-4-0s and 'M7' 0-4-4Ts were found at many sheds and hence would be seen over much of the system. Conversely classes like the 'O298' Beattie 2-4-0 well tanks were generally restricted to a particular stretch of line, in this case the Wenford Bridge freight branch east of Wadebridge. Hence it would be unusual (though not, of course, impossible) for one of these 2-4-0WTs to appear on, say, a layout based on somewhere in the Bournemouth area. It would not be typical of the area and thus it would make the layout less effective than it need be.

Right; you've decided to model the Western Section of the Southern in the late 1940s/early 1950s. What sort of balanced locomotive stud is required? Much depends on which part of the area you want to feature. The section can be broadly divided into three groups:

Nine Elms

Group:	Nine Elms	
	Feltham	250 locomotives
	Guildford	
	Basingstoke	

Eastleigh

Group:	Eastleigh	
	Fratton	
	Southampton	273 locomotives
	Bournemouth	
	Dorchester	

Exmouth Junction

Group:	Salisbury	
	Templecombe	
	Yeovil	
	Exmouth Junction	238 locomotives
	Barnstaple	
	Plymouth	
	Wadebridge	

Now by calculating the percentage of each type of wheel arrangement in each of these three groups we get the following result:

Group	Nine Elms	Eastleigh	Exmouth Junction
Wheel Arrangement			
4-6-2	11%	3%	21%
4-6-0	27%	16%	12%
4-4-0	12%	30%	13%
2-6-0	7%	4%	15%
0-6-0	19%	11%	4%
4-8-0T	2%	Nil	Nil
0-8-0T	1%	1%	1%
4-6-2T	2%	Nil	Nil
0-6-2T	2%	4%	5%
0-6-0T	4%	11%	1%
4-4-2T	Nil	Nil	1%
2-4-0T	Nil	Nil	1%
0-4-4T	12%	17%	24%
0-4-0T	1%	3%	2%

At a glance we can see the proportion of types allocated to an area. The most numerous type in the Nine Elms group being 4-6-0s, in the Eastleigh group it is 4-4-0s whilst further west around Exmouth Junction it is the 0-4-4T. Assuming one has 10 locomotives, here is my suggestion for a balanced stud for a model layout based in each of these three areas:

Nine Elms Group

4-6-2 – 1 'Merchant Navy'
4-6-0 – 3 'H15', 'N15', 'S15'
4-4-0 – 1 'T9'
2-6-0 – 1 'U'
0-6-0 – 2 '700', 'Q1'

SOUTHERN STEAM — WESTERN SECTION ALLOCATIONS (August 1950)

Class	Wadebridge	Plymouth	Barnstaple	Exmouth Junction	Yeovil	Templecombe	Salisbury	Dorchester	Bournemouth	Southampton	Fratton	Eastleigh	Basingstoke	Guildford	Feltham	Nine Elms	
BB									1							17	4-6-2
MN																12	
WC		4		30	4	5	7										
H15										12			2		2	12	
LN						5				8						3	
N15			2			10	3			11	2		1		1	11	4-6-0
N15X													7				
S15			10			7									28		
T14													3		2		
B4X									10								
D15															1	1	
K10			2	3				3	13		2	4			4		4-4-0
L11				1	2		1	4	8	1		4					
L12						1	3	5	1								
S11			9	4	10	4	1	14	14	2	4	2		2	7		
T9									2								
K		1	1	22				1	3								2-6-0
N				5	4		3	3	2	1	12	1		5			
U							2		4								
C3									8								
Q					2				9		8	8					0-6-0
Q1						5	1		4	2	4	9		5			
700			2			1			2		7	6					
0395									4								
G16				1		1			3						1		4-8-0T
Z															5		0-8-0T
H16		1	5	4					1	3	1				3		4-6-2T
E1/R		2															
E4					5			2	3	2	1				1		0-6-2T
757								2	1	1	2	3			3		
A1X					3					1							
E1										14							
G6	3																0-4-2T
P															4		2-4-0T
USA			5	7	24	2		5	14	4	15		11	2	12		
0415	2	5	6				6	2	3						1		4-4-2T
0298	1							1	1								
H	4							3	3								
M7									2						1		0-4-4T

0-4-4T – 1 'M7'
plus 1 other

Eastleigh Group
4-6-0 – 2 'Lord Nelson', 'N15'
4-4-0 – 3 'L11', 'T9', 'T9'
0-6-0 – 1 'Q'
0-6-0T – 1 'E1'
0-4-4T – 2 'M7'
plus 1 other

Exmouth Junction Group
4-6-2 – 2 'West Country'
4-6-0 – 1 'S15'
4-4-0 – 1 'T9'
2-6-0 – 2 'N'
0-4-4T – 3 'M7', '02'
plus 1 other

Left:
The 10.38 mixed train from Halwill Junction-Torrington waits time at Yarde halt. The date is 3 June 1959 and the locomotive an Ivatt '2MT' 2-6-2T. *J. H. Aston*

SOUTHERN STEAM – Western Section models available

Class	'N' RTR	'N' KIT	'TT' RTR	'TT' KIT	'00' RTR	'00' KIT	'O' RTR	'O' KIT
BB	1	–	–	–	1	3	–	–
MN	1	1	3	–	–	1	–	–
WC	1	–	–	–	1	3	–	–
H15	–	–	–	–	–	1	–	–
LN	–	–	–	–	–	1	–	–
N15	–	1	–	–	2	1	–	–
N15X	–	–	–	–	–	1	–	–
S15	–	1	–	–	–	1	–	–
T14	–	–	–	–	–	1	–	–
B4X	–	–	–	–	–	–	–	–
D15	–	–	–	–	–	1	–	–
K10	–	–	–	–	–	–	–	–
L11	–	–	–	–	–	–	–	–
L12	–	–	–	–	–	1	–	–
S11	–	–	–	–	–	–	–	–
T9	–	–	–	–	–	1	–	–
K	–	–	–	–	–	1	–	–
N	–	–	–	–	–	1	–	–
U	–	–	–	–	–	1	–	–
C3	–	–	–	–	–	–	–	–
Q	–	–	–	–	–	1	–	–
Q1	–	1	–	–	–	1	–	1
700	–	–	–	–	–	3	–	–
0395	–	–	–	–	–	1	–	–
G16	–	–	–	–	–	–	–	–
Z	–	–	–	–	–	–	–	–
H16	–	–	–	–	–	–	–	–
E1/R	–	–	–	–	–	–	–	–
E4	–	–	–	–	–	–	–	–
757	–	–	–	–	–	–	–	–
A1X	–	–	–	–	–	1	–	1
E1	–	–	–	–	–	1	–	–
G6	–	–	–	3	–	1	–	–
P	–	–	–	–	–	1	–	–
USA	–	–	–	–	–	1	–	–
0415	–	–	–	–	–	1	–	–
0298	–	–	–	–	–	2	–	1
H	–	–	–	–	–	1	–	1
M7	–	–	–	–	3	1	–	1
02	–	–	–	–	–	1	–	–
T1	–	–	–	–	–	1	–	1
B4	–	1	–	–	–	1	–	–
C14	–	–	–	–	–	–	–	–
0458	–	–	–	–	–	–	–	–

Notes : 1 = Currently advertised as available or for future release.

2 = Recently discontinued but may still be obtained albeit at an inflated price.

3 = Discontinued a number of years ago but sometimes seen on the secondhand market.

Finally a brief look at models available for the Western Section of the Southern. Only in 4mm scale is the area reasonably represented in terms of models as the table shows. Ready-to-run (RTR) equipment is very sparse and one has to resort to kit building to build up a varied stud of locomotives. At the time of writing only the 'Battle of Britain'/'West Country' class is available in any scale in ready-to-run form. I'm excluding the Hornby 'Schools' class as this was not allocated to the Western Section in 1950.

Only Tri-ang and its successor Hornby have really been interested in the Southern. Perhaps one day of the other major manufacturers will turn away from the current GWR/LMS mixture and have a look at the railway which operated south of the Thames.

Above:
Ex-LSWR 'T9' 4-4-0 No 30712 departs Padstow with a stopping train for Launceston composed of the standard Maunsell two-coach set. *B. A. Butt*

Below:
'N' class 2-6-0 No 31838 heads a typical short freight from Exeter-Ilfracombe near Mortehoe in September 1959. *Derek Cross*

Above:
West Country motive power. 'Battle of Britain' 4-6-2 No 34069 *Hawkinge* arrives at Wadebridge with a passenger train as Beattie 2-4-0WT No 30586 shunts in the yard.
M. J. Esau

Left:
Adams 'O2' 0-4-4T No 30183 waits with the branch mixed train at Callington on 17 June 1959.
G. M. Kichenside

Below left:
Another view of Wadebridge with 'N' 2-6-0 No 31830 on the 09.56 Okehampton-Padstow on 3 July 1962. *B. S. Jennings*

Right:
'M7' 0-4-4T No 30356 heads an Exeter-Exmouth working on 21 August 1951. *D. Clark*

Below right:
A typical Waterloo-Plymouth train of the early 1960s formed of assorted BR Mk 1 and Maunsell stock headed by Rebuilt 'Battle of Britain' No 34056 *Croydon* is seen at Exeter St Davids on 27 July 1961. *P. J. Hurcum*

Below:
More familiar on freight work, but sometimes used on local passenger turns were the 'S15' 4-6-0s. No 30830 heads a local to Exeter at Seaton Junction on 14 June 1963. *R. Hewitt*

Above:
'West Country' 4-6-2 No 34107 *Blandford Forum* climbs out of Buckhorn Weston tunnel with a long mixed freight on 20 March 1962. *R. T. Hughes*

Right:
A Class H freight bound for Plymouth Friary enters Mutley tunnel behind 'N' class 2-6-0 No 31847, a type much used in the West of England during the twilight years of steam. *R. E. Vincent*

Below:
A veteran of many years in the far west, 'T9' 4-4-0 No 30338 stands on the Padstow turntable on 14 June 1960. *K. R. Pirt*

Scenic Casting Rural Boundary Walls

Eric Taylor

There are several methods available on the market to facilitate home moulding of various scenic items. But, when I started doing 'my own thing' some 30 years ago, the only material that seemed to produce a constant result every time was Vinamold Hot Melt Compound. This is available in a variety of melting temperatures – coded by the material's colour.

Red is the lowest melting at 130-150°C (248-302°F) and is graded as medium soft. There is another grade that is softer, but it melts at the upper extreme. Thus, while the softer, more pliable mould is desirable, in that it exerts less strain on the cast during removal, the red compound is quite soft enough in the sizes used by modellers, and it melts at a reasonable temperature.

As a guide when deciding how much to obtain, 1lb of Vinamold equals 27.5 cubic in (450 cu cm) approximately.

There was also a moulding latex which I found was comparatively harder than the Hot Melt Compound, took longer to build up a coating over the pattern, and was generally less flexible – especially where the parts to be cast were more delicate. I still use it on the odd occasion for very small, plain casts where any detail is on a flat surface. Though it is rubber, it is not as elastic as Vinamold.

Later in my use of this material, I started making the odd railway item here and there – including walls. The one thing that made them look better than the shop bought wall section was that, being cast in plaster, they had a natural stone texture that was missing in the metal or plastic walls available at model shops.

Two things happened over the years between. I used to cast my parts in Dental Stone (EP1) which was far harder (and still is) than Plaster of Paris, which in those days, was very gritty and had the strength of chalk. To me, Dental Stone has priced itself out of my reach (the last price rise was in the area of 65%). But, over the same time period, there has been an improvement in the quality of Plaster of Paris (there are several grades) and now a very good impression can be taken from a mould and it has adequate strength for modelwork. The grade I use is called casting plaster. Of course, this too has risen in price gradually, but is far cheaper than Dental Stone. The beauty of Dental Stone was its rapid setting time. A cast could be removed from the mould some 20 min after pouring. The Plaster of Paris needs to be left at least 45-60 min for plain surfaced casts or, 1½ hr if it contains undercuts or fine projections.

With planning ahead, plaster casts can be made at odd spare times and left to be removed at the next spare moment or two. Do not use 'Builders Grade' plaster as used for wall joints, crack filler etc. This is the cheapest grade and is not so fine in texture. Both casting plaster and Dental Stone have minimal expansion on setting.

With the commercially produced wall sections the straight-line joint between each length is so obvious, that, short of covering each joint with shrubbery at regular spacings, or a buttress pillar, the joint stood out like the proverbial sore thumb. Later, it will be seen how this was overcome.

To produce repetition casting, a mould is needed. To make a mould, first a pattern is required. The following, while describing rural boundary walls is the same method as used for most items, though some, being only one-sided, will require a slightly different technique.

These may be found along many country roads, round farm buildings and so on. There are slight variations from one district to another, such as the height, and thickness, type of stone used, whether the stone is dressed or in the rough and, the type of capping to the wall, if any. Generally, where this type of wall is used, it would take an expert to say that the type of wall shown on one scene does not belong in that area. To 99% of the viewers, one random stone wall will look just like any other,

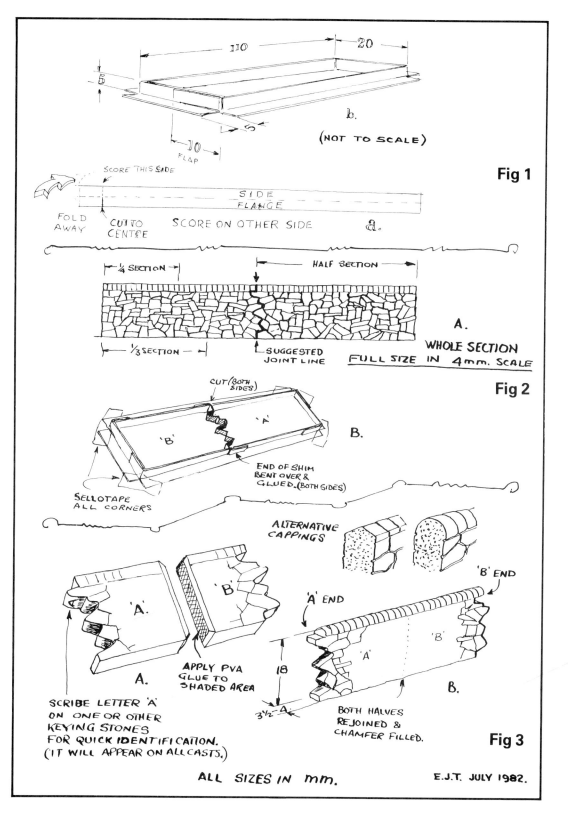

110

20

5

b.

(NOT TO SCALE)

10
FLAP

5

Fig 1

SCORE THIS SIDE

SIDE
FLANGE

FOLD AWAY

CUT TO CENTRE

SCORE ON OTHER SIDE

a.

¼ SECTION

HALF SECTION

⅓ SECTION

SUGGESTED JOINT LINE

A.

WHOLE SECTION
FULL SIZE IN 4mm. SCALE

Fig 2

CUT (BOTH SIDES)

'A'

'B'

B.

END OF SHIM BENT OVER & GLUED. (BOTH SIDES)

SELLOTAPE ALL CORNERS

ALTERNATIVE CAPPINGS

'A'

'B'

APPLY PVA GLUE TO SHADED AREA

A.

SCRIBE LETTER 'A' ON ONE OR OTHER KEYING STONES FOR QUICK IDENTIFICATION. (IT WILL APPEAR ON ALL CASTS.)

'A' END

'B' END

'A'

'B'

18

3½

BOTH HALVES REJOINED & CHAMFER FILLED.

B.

Fig 3

ALL SIZES IN mm.

E.J.T. JULY 1982.

unless it definitely should be a dry stone type.

These walls are, *on average*, some 4ft 6in high, by 10in-12in thick. Usually, they are topped by a course of capping stones or bricks, either of triangular section giving a gabled top, or of half-round section.

In 4mm scale, I found that approximately scale 25ft lengths (100mm) were a convenient size for many long runs of wall. By also making them in half, quarter and one third lengths, a combination can be used to suit the overall length required.

The Pattern

Starting with the whole section length of wall, we need a plain slab of plaster 110mm × 20mm × 5mm. When this is dressed down, it will finish at 110mm × 18mm × 3½-4mm thick. It looks more realistic if the thickness does vary between 3½-4mm.

To start, cut two strips of thin card (cereal packets will do) 120mm × 10mm and score with the point of a knife down the centre (5mm from each edge). Next, score across 10mm from one end,

Below:
Retainer for pattern.

on the opposite side of the card. Cut right through on one side of the centre line and fold out away from the scored line both ways. The 10mm length is a gluing tab. Cut two lengths 30mm × 10mm. Repeat the scoring as before, leaving each piece now 20mm, plus the 10mm gluing tab (see **Fig 1A**). Glue the four pieces together to form a rectangle with a flange for gluing down to a plate. This must be as flat as possible. I prefer to use either a sheet of Paxolin board or a glass plate (see **Fig 1B**). After gluing the flange to the plate, add a short strip of Sellotape over each corner where there may still be a tiny gap.

This container, filled with plaster, would give the required size of slab, but with straight line ends.

Fig 2A shows a square-ended panel of wall in random stone. Cut a strip of 5thou shim brass to no less than the depth of the card retainer walls – and about 50-60mm long. At one end of the shim strip, bend about 10mm round to 90° so that it will stand on its own edge. Lay it over the wall diagram in **Fig 2A** – about the middle and where there is a convenient series of stone joints from top to bottom. With some pointed-nosed pliers, bend the shim to follow the joint line selected. Ensure that all the bends are square to the strip – so that one edge will sit flat on a plate.

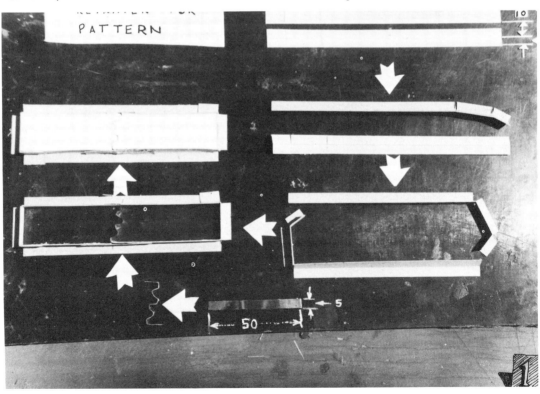

Make a clean cut down both long sides of the retainer – about in the middle and insert the shim into this slot. Bend the spare ends over against the outside and glue another strip of card over them – mainly to strengthen the cut sides.

(Fig 2B) Mark the right hand side **A**, and the left side **B**. Ensure that the lower edge of the shim is in contact with the base plate.

Mix some casting plaster in an old cup – to a very thick cream texture. Allow a few minutes for it to 'work' and for air bubbles to rise, while it is moved about with a teaspoon. Apply a spoonful each side of the shim and, by working with the spoon, ease it into the contours on both sides. Add more plaster to each half and by dabbing with the spoon, work it into the corners of the card retainer. Level it off flush with the top and allow it an hour to set.

When hard, pick away the card retainer and, before removing the plaster slab from the board, scribe some joint lines of stones each side of the shim divider. Insert a thin knife blade under the edge of the set plaster – a little at a time until it lifts off the board. The chances are that it will separate at the shim but just fit the halves together, turn it over and scribe stone joint lines on that side also about

Below:
Steps in producing the master wall section.

the shim joint. (This ensures that stones on each side of the joint match up together.)

Now, separate the two pieces, remove the shim strip and change both pieces end for end – so that **A** is now on the left hand side. Dress the smooth joints square by holding against a square block of wood and rubbing the ends on a sheet of sandpaper. When done, add about a 1mm chamfer to the joint corners all round as in **Fig 3A**. Apply glue (when plaster is really set, in about 3-4hr, to the flat end of the joint only and glue both halves together on a flat surface. With a small painting brush, add more plaster to the chamfers and fill them up all round. Smooth it off flush with the surface.

Hold the whole wall panel against the wood block and square off the bottom edge of the wall. Turn over, and straighten out any deformity in the top edge. While in this position, the wall may be rocked from side to side during each rubbing stroke to impart a rounded top for the capping stones, or, held at a constant angle to form a gabled top (**Fig 3B**). It will now be seen that there is a whole wall section with keyed ends that will fit another length if mated to it the same way round. From this point we will refer to the ends as **A** end and **B** end. It will be seen that any wall section will fit another by mating an **A** end with a **B** end, but not an **A** end to

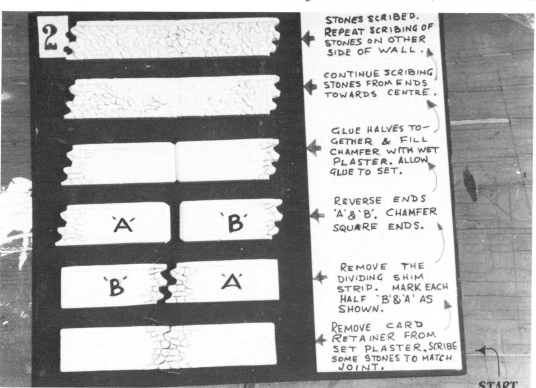

STONES SCRIBED.
REPEAT SCRIBING OF
STONES ON OTHER
SIDE OF WALL.

CONTINUE SCRIBING
STONES FROM ENDS
TOWARDS CENTRE.

GLUE HALVES TO-
GETHER & FILL
CHAMFER WITH WET
PLASTER. ALLOW
GLUE TO SET.

REVERSE ENDS
'A' & 'B'. CHAMFER
SQUARE ENDS.

REMOVE THE
DIVIDING SHIM
STRIP. MARK EACH
HALF 'B' & 'A' AS
SHOWN.

REMOVE CARD
RETAINER FROM
SET PLASTER. SCRIBE
SOME STONES TO MATCH
JOINT.

START

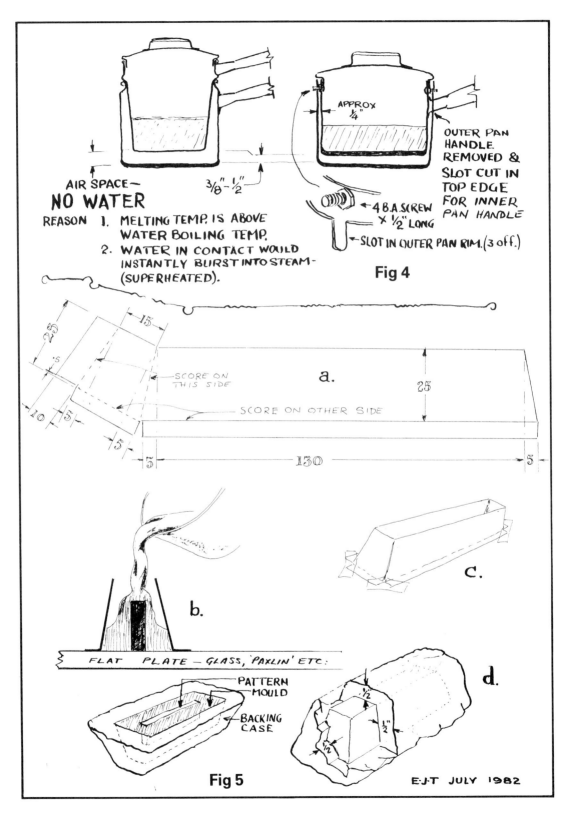

AIR SPACE—
NO WATER
REASON 1. MELTING TEMP. IS ABOVE
WATER BOILING TEMP.
2. WATER IN CONTACT WOULD
INSTANTLY BURST INTO STEAM—
(SUPERHEATED).

3/8" - 1/2"

APPROX 1/4"

OUTER PAN HANDLE. REMOVED & SLOT CUT IN TOP EDGE FOR INNER PAN HANDLE

4 B.A. SCREW X 1/2" LONG

SLOT IN OUTER PAN RIM. (3 off.)

Fig 4

25
15
·5
SCORE ON THIS SIDE
10
5
5
5
130
5

a.

25

SCORE ON OTHER SIDE

b.

FLAT PLATE — GLASS, 'PAXLIN' ETC.

c.

d.

1/2
1/2
1/2

PATTERN MOULD
BACKING CASE

Fig 5

E·J·T JULY 1982

104

another **A** end. Thus, when a length of walling is being assembled, the sections must be turned the right way round to fit.

Once casts have been made of this section, some can be cut to half, third and quarter lengths, rejoined as described above and moulds made so that it is possible to mould any length needed. All will have the same keying at the ends and so can be inserted into a wall at any point.

It remains to scribe in the rest of the random stones working in from those already started at the original joints. It is not really necessary to follow the pattern shown in Fig 2A as random stone means just that; stones picked up at random and not selected.

When all the stones have been scribed in on both sides of the wall panel, it should then be air dried for several hours before being placed in a cold oven and the heat brought up gradually to about 150°F (65·5°C). Leave it in there for an hour or two at that heat, then turn the oven off and allow to cool. It is now ready to be used as the first wall pattern.

Making the Mould

When obtaining the Vinamold Hot Melt Compound, Code No 1028 red, ensure that the leaflet issued with it from the manufacturers Vinetex Ltd, Carshalton, Surrey, England, is also collected. It contains some very informative material on how to use the various grades of Vinamold.

Briefly, the compound must be cut up into small pieces to enable it to melt as quickly as possible. It should be heated in a double container to prevent it

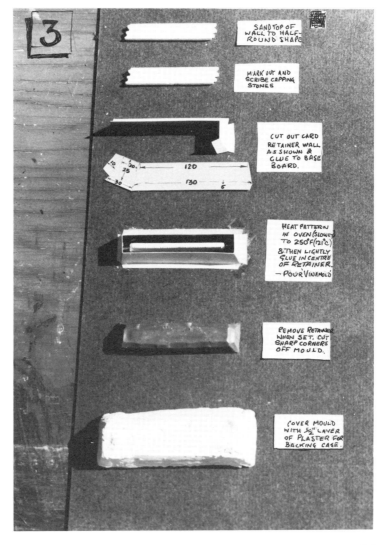

Right:
Making the mould.

105

burning – or perhaps more correctly, overheating. **Fig 4A** shows the type of container required: an old double boiler, or two saucepans adapted. There should be a minimum of ⅜in-½in between the bottom of the inner and outer containers. No water is to be used between – just air space. Do not apply too much heat. There are vapours that come off the melting of the compound, but these will be seen to be different from the blue smoke that occurs when the heat is too great. Too much heat also causes the material to lose its oils and its flexibility. It will also change from a bright red to a light chocolate brown.

I can only state the electric stove regulator figures. I have found the best results are obtained by initially melting at No 3 (hotplate setting) – then reducing to between No 3 and No 2. If any delay requires the material to be held in that state for a short time, lower the setting to just below No 2. Where some hotplates are not numbered, they may have marks such as 'Low', 'Medium' and 'High'. The comparable settings will be found to be just below No 3 (Medium) and about the same as No 2 (Low). As in many other new attempts at something, the trial and error method will have to be adopted in the first instance.

I mentioned that there will be vapours coming off the melting compound, so, it should be done at a time when the 'Boss of the kitchen' is out for the day, (or has gone home to Mum). It makes a good excuse to get a venting fan fitted over the stove, or, secondly, use a portable hot-plate out in the shed. I should add that the vapours are rather sickly – so keep away from the open saucepan.

In between the times that more small quantities of Vinamold are being added to the pot for melting, mark and cut out a card retainer as shown in **Fig 5A**. The 5mm flange is glued down to the flat surface and the same 10mm tabs are used as in the much shallower retainer made for the plaster slab. It will be seen that this time the sides are tapered inwards to the top. The dimensions given apply mainly to the clearance round the pattern. The principle will apply to all future retainers – just the sizes will differ. (See **Fig 5 A, B, & C**).

At the same time that the compound is being melted, place the pattern on a shelf in the middle area of the oven, turn the bottom heater on as low as possible for 10 min, then raise it gradually to 250°F. It may be a good time to remind users that the plaster was mixed with water in the first place. The structure is a mass of minute air spaces – with a percentage of moisture still retained in the surrounding structure. Therefore, it will be seen

that as soon as heat is applied suddenly, when the compound is poured over the pattern, the heat will force out more moisture in the form of steam and air bubbles. These do nothing for the accuracy and finish of the mould surfaces. Some of the bubbles get trapped in the compound close to the pattern surface and, even if not actually breaking the surface, they cause the mould to be 'spongy' and distort under the weight of the plaster. It is not much use making a mould round a pattern if the result will not reproduce the shape required, due to its weakness.

Over the years, I have tried all kinds of methods to seal patterns so that no bubbles are forced out during the mould pouring. When using a plaster pattern, I have yet to find a better way than to heat the pattern to near the same temperature as the hot compound. If anything this has the tendency to hold the mould material tighter to the pattern and produces few if any trapped bubbles.

When the compound has been melted, and the pattern heated to the same temperature, take it out of the oven, apply a dab of PVA glue to the bottom of the wall and set it perpendicular on the board in the middle of the retainer. Pour the hot material over the pattern. It will run into all indents, crevices and corners, until the retainer is full to the top. Keeping the board level, allow the mould to set for a couple of hours.

Backing Case

When set, remove the retainer. With scissors or a sharp and wet knife, cut the sharp corners off the outside of the mould. Now, mix a cup full of plaster to a thick consistency. Apply it to the top of the mould as it stands on the board and spread it over until the mould is covered to a depth of about ½in **(Fig 5D)**. Leave it to set for an hour or so and then remove it by inserting a knife blade between it and the board. It may be that the whole thing will come off in one piece.

The ½in thick coating of plaster over the mould is a backing case to hold it in shape while pouring further casts. Being a soft and flexible material, it would tend to sag or adopt the contours of the surface on which it is standing. Therefore a backing of plaster is always added over the mould before it is removed from the board.

Remove the mould from the backing case. The original pattern may, or may not, come out in one piece. Do not worry if it does not. If there is anything unsatisfactory with the finish of the first cast made, it will serve as a pattern with the adjustments required. When the pattern has been taken out, make a clean straight cut down each end of the mould – flush with one edge of the end of the wall – as shown in **Fig 5E**. However flexible the mould material is, there are a series of undercuts involved with the 'keyed' ends of the wall section. In a fully hard state, the mould could be pulled off these undercuts, but, in the condition of the plaster when it is only just set, it is asking too much. The keyed end stones will be broken. So, by making a clean-line cut as shown, the mould can be folded open after it is taken out of the backing case, and peeled back from the new cast item. It is necessary for a clean-line cut to be made so that the opposing edges fit together in the right place when it is put back into the backing case. We have all seen the result of a cast part where the mould halves have been cut off line.

Casting

Have you ever concreted a path, or seen it done? Where a good strong surface was required, it may have been noted that the mixture was in a fairly thick texture, but after smoothing off, it was sprayed with a fine mist of water to delay the drying time. Once set enough, wet sacking may have been spread over it to further delay the loss of moisture. The less water added to a concrete mix, the quicker it will set. The quicker the setting, the more stresses are induced into it, and the greater the risk of cracking.

At the same time, a less wet mix is stronger than a thin, watery brew. So, by mixing a batch of concrete with less water, but delaying the setting time by keeping it wet, one gains the best of both worlds.

This applies equally to the plaster mix needed for these castings. Mix just enough for the number of moulds that can be filled before setting begins and, mix the plaster to a consistency that will allow it to be poured into the mould and worked into all the corners and undercuts but, allow it to set as slowly as possible. It is only partly set when it is hard enough to be removed from the mould. It will not be fully set for at least 12-18 hr. Even then it is not 'cured' for some four days – though it is well set for our use after a day.

When the cast is removed from the mould, (the time will depend on the consistency of the mix and

Below:
The finished mould.

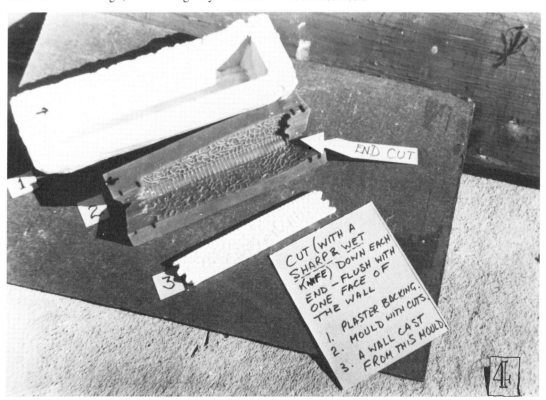

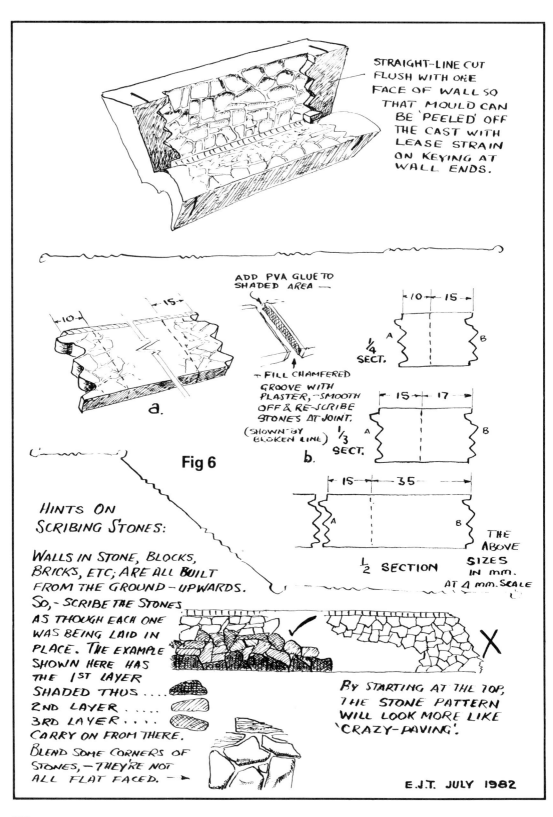

STRAIGHT-LINE CUT FLUSH WITH ONE FACE OF WALL SO THAT MOULD CAN BE 'PEELED' OFF THE CAST WITH LEASE STRAIN ON KEYING AT WALL ENDS.

ADD PVA GLUE TO SHADED AREA —

FILL CHAMFERED GROOVE WITH PLASTER, — SMOOTH OFF & RE-SCRIBE STONES AT JOINT. (SHOWN BY BROKEN LINE)

a.

b.

Fig 6

¼ SECT.

A   10   15   B

⅓ SECT.

A   15   17   B

½ SECTION

A   15   35   B

THE ABOVE SIZES IN mm. AT 4 mm. SCALE

HINTS ON SCRIBING STONES:

WALLS IN STONE, BLOCKS, BRICKS, ETC; ARE ALL BUILT FROM THE GROUND — UPWARDS. SO, — SCRIBE THE STONES AS THOUGH EACH ONE WAS BEING LAID IN PLACE. THE EXAMPLE SHOWN HERE HAS THE 1ST LAYER SHADED THUS ....

2ND LAYER .....

3RD LAYER ....

CARRY ON FROM THERE.

BLEND SOME CORNERS OF STONES, — THEY'RE NOT ALL FLAT FACED. —➤

BY STARTING AT THE TOP, THE STONE PATTERN WILL LOOK MORE LIKE 'CRAZY-PAVING'.

E.J.T. JULY 1982

by trial and error) it should not be force dried as it will lose its moisture unevenly and crack. It should be laid on a non-absorbent surface, away from draughts for at least two-three hours. It may then be put on a folded newspaper for as long as can be spared. In the case of these small wall sections, they do not bear any stress when installed on the layout scene. After a few hours, the cast will be hard enough to be painted and if necessary, added to the scenery.

Let us return to the beginning – before the plaster was poured into the mould.

Remove the mould from its case, pull it open to check that there are no grains of already set plaster left in it. Rinse it under running water and add no more than two drips of washing-up liquid, rinse it about and pour off. This ensures a good wet surface inside the mould. The plaster will creep by capillary action into even tiny cracks or scratches and produce an accurate reproduction of the mould surface. Replace the mould in its backing case ensuring that the cut ends are lined up. Now the plaster can be poured.

That is the basic method of reproduction casting of an often used item of rural scenery. But, it need not end there. The foregoing may sound like a very complicated operation. The first time it is done, it may not be quite as complicated as it sounds. Then, in subsequent attempts, it will be found more easy the more often it is done. I find it is the best way to produce a lot of the same thing and now I have lost count of the number of moulds I have made. The good feature of Vinamold is that, once it is finished with, the mould can be cut up and re-melted for some other item.

I always keep a good casting from a mould as a pattern for future use. The odd occasion does turn up where one thinks that a particular job is finally finished with. Then, at some later date, the same thing is wanted again. Without keeping a sample cast, it would be necessary to start from scratch again, but with a cast on hand, it can be used as a

Below:
Removing a cast from the mould.

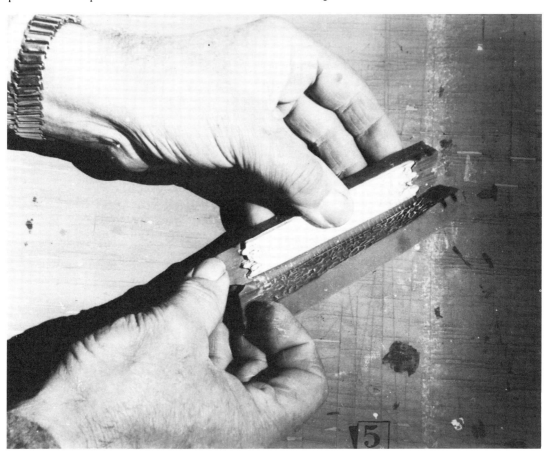

pattern. The Vinamold does not seem to lose its texture over a long period. I have moulds in use now that were made over 20 years ago. I must say, though, that if I had to make a new one to replace them, they would have a further 20 years knowledge of making patterns added to their design.

As mentioned at the start of this article, these wall sections could also be made in half, quarter or third lengths for adaptation to the length required. To do this, it is suggested that three or four casts be made for cutting up for the patterns of the smaller sections. This way, the same keying is used on the wall ends, ensuring that all sections of any length will fit to any other.

In this method, a whole section cast is taken and, when set, a clean saw cut is made vertically up the wall some 10-15mm from one end (Fig 6A). A second cut is made in from the other end to a length so that when the two are glued together as described for joining the original length, they make up the length of section required (Fig 6B).

Rural boundary walls are not always just plain lengths from A to B. They must start somewhere and end at another point. These ends do not show rough random stones. They are usually finished in a vertical row of dressed stone or a brick column. This can be done by cutting a section off square and painting a strip up the end with wet plaster on a brush. When it is dry, dressed stones can be scribed on the new end. It can be used as a pattern. Remember that there is also an end **B** needed, as well as end **A** (Fig 7A).

In addition to wall ends, one will often find there is a junction where one wall may go off to the right or left. At times, these walls also make up divisions of farm yards, pig styes etc. Here one finds a cruciform section (**Fig 7C**). Then, one comes to the corner of a property. The wall may continue to right or left as the geography demands (**Fig 7D**). Lastly, don't forget where the wall curves into the gateway of the Squire's country mansion (**Fig 7E**).

All these sections can easily be made up from ends of wall sections, glued together and used as before as patterns. In the case of the curved sections, it is necessary to add short straight sections between the keyed ends and blend the sudden angular change into a curve. There is one short section that I found came in handy. This was a short piece with the same keying on both ends. It may be found that due to intersections and junctions, one finds a change in the direction of the keying pattern. This piece corrects the problem (**Fig 7F**).

Below:
Wall sections and assembly arrangements.

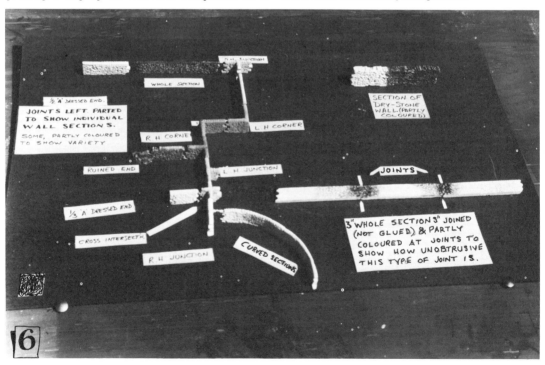

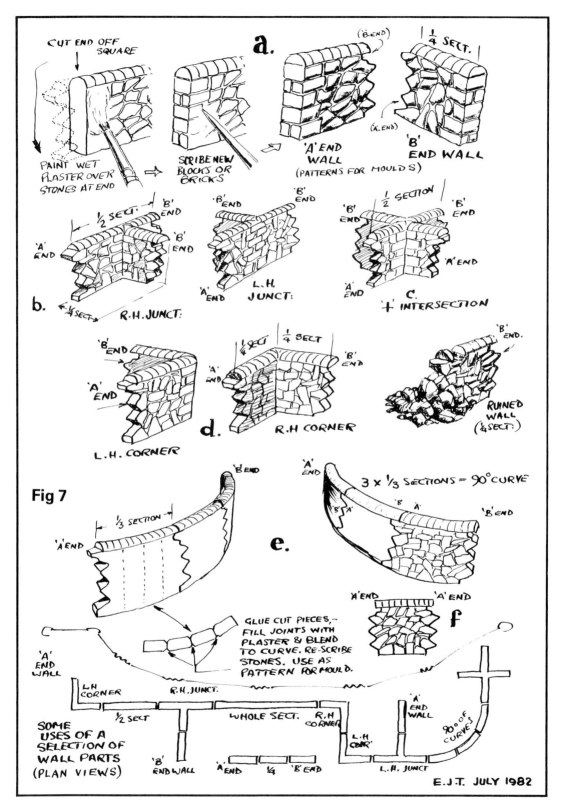

a. CUT END OFF SQUARE — PAINT WET PLASTER OVER STONES AT END → SCRIBE NEW BLOCKS OR BRICKS → 'A' END WALL (PATTERNS FOR MOULDS) — 'B' END WALL ('B.END') ('A.END') — ¼ SECT.

b. R.H. JUNCT: ('B' END, 'A' END, ½ SECT, ¼ SECT) — L.H. JUNCT: ('B' END, 'A' END) — **c.** 'T' INTERSECTION ('B' END, ½ SECTION, 'B' END, 'A' END)

d. L.H. CORNER ('B' END, 'A' END) — R.H. CORNER (¼ SECT, 'A' END, 'B' END) — RUINED WALL (¼ SECT:) ('B' END)

Fig 7

e. ⅓ SECTION ('A' END, 'B' END) — 3 × ⅓ SECTIONS = 90° CURVE ('A' END, 'B' 'A', 'B' 'A', 'B' END) — GLUE CUT PIECES, — FILL JOINTS WITH PLASTER & BLEND TO CURVE. RE-SCRIBE STONES. USE AS PATTERN FOR MOULD.

f. ('A' END, 'A' END)

SOME USES OF A SELECTION OF WALL PARTS (PLAN VIEWS)

'A' END WALL — L.H. CORNER — R.H. JUNCT. — ½ SECT — WHOLE SECT. — R.H. CORNER — L.H. CORNR — 'A' END WALL — 90° OF CURVES — 'B' END WALL — 'A' END — ¼ — 'B' END — L.H. JUNCT

E.J.T. JULY 1982

Endless Rope Wagon Haulage

G. A. Hope

(EM Gauge Society)

An article appeared in the December 1977, *MRC* outlining various methods of rope haulage. The author, D. R. Thornton, indicated a need for an answer to the problem of clamping and releasing wagons to grip the rope in the endless rope system. This got me thinking.

I know nothing about narrow gauge or contractors' railways, but such problems are like a red rag to a bull in my eyes. The method I devised was to use a steel wire cable of a type sometimes used for needle movement in radio sets. Secondly, an electromagnet mounted in the wagons being moved acts as a clamp. A current being passed through the coil of the magnet will cause the cable to be gripped strongly enough to enable the hauling of the wagon to the other end of the system. A motor, suitably geared, can then decide the speed at which the wagon moves.

The method of getting the power to the magnet, obviously is to treat the wagon as a locomotive with no wheel drive. Current collection is necessary on all four wheels, since the grip on the rope must, at all times during the wagon's progress, be absolutely certain. Also, cleanliness of track and wheels is essential for proper working, especially if there is a gradient involved.

Now, such a method of attacking the problem must be accompanied by a suitable means of separating the moving vehicles, or so Mr. Thornton indicates. In this case, we must prevent a second wagon attaching itself to the cable immediately after the first has cleared the clamping point. This can be achieved by use of a relay and track sectioning.

The diagram shows that the track is divided into 'store', 'grip', 'spacer', 'main haul' and 'release' sections. The relay **A** has but one contact, a changeover. The motor, of course, is permanently wired to the power supply switch, as is the relay.

With the circuit 'at rest' (no wagons on line), current supply is available on sections **2**, **3** (via the relay coil) and **4**. If the store section is on a slight gradient, the first wagon can be made to run onto the grip section, where its magnet will operate, so gripping the cable. The wagon will then be hauled to section **3**. On touching this section, it will cause the relay to operate and the changeover contact to cut the supply to the grip section. The 'make' side of the changeover puts a resistor (**R**) into parallel with the relay coil, thus supplying sufficient power to maintain the magnet grip. The reason for the resistor is to provide the power without short circuiting the relay, which must remain in operation until the leading wagon has cleared the spacer section, which is the active faction in the spacing facility. When the wagon clears this section, the relay, since it relies on the presence of a load on the track, releases, thus returning power to the grip section, where the next wagon is waiting. The process then begins again.

At the other end of the line, wagons run onto the release section **5**, where current for the magnet is not available. The magnet is de-energised and the wagon is thus freed to go, or be taken, to its destination.

If there is any change of gradient over the line, I would suggest that the wagon magnets are mounted on a pivoting arm so as to take up any vertical movement. A bottom limit stop should be fitted to prevent the magnet falling below rail level.

The relay coil resistance should be in the region 200-400 ohms. The resistor being of 12-15 ohms value at 5W rating.

Now, to the cost of the installation. As with most electrical installations, energy is the biggest wallet breaker. Having furnished the system with wire cable, pulleys, motor and relay as well as the magnet in each wagon, we find that, due to the number of wagons being hauled, the consumption of juice will be quite high. Suppose each wagon takes 0.5A to power its magnet. This may involve the builder in a power pack of at least 5A delivery current. It may be possible to make or buy magnets that take less current. I don't know, but here, at least, is one answer to the problem.

As you may gather from all this, I have not experimented on it myself. I am much too busy trying to get my own layout into working order. If my article has done its job, there should be some jokers getting down to the nitty gritty and aiming to be the first with a working model. Come on, chaps, I leave it to you.

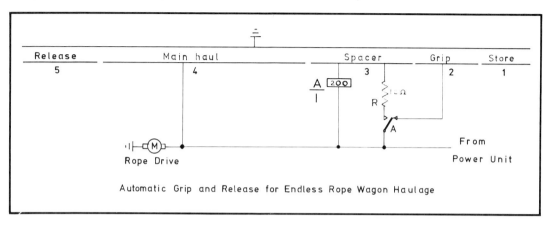

Automatic Grip and Release for Endless Rope Wagon Haulage

Below:
Rope wagon haulage as demonstrated on the preserved Bowes Railway in Tyne & Wear. *I. S. Carr*

Hand-built Trackwork in 4mm Scale

Eric W. J. Walford

These days a growing number of people are turning their hand to making their own trackwork and finding it remarkably simple in the process. This article deals with one of a number of good methods which can be used and is aimed primarily at those who have never made their own track before, although it may also be useful to those who are 'old hands'. The method I am going to outline was first shown to me some 12 years ago and above all else, requires patience, a commodity which is always useful. Without it, you should not be in the hobby anyway. At the rate of one foot per hour, (or thereabouts), it takes a fair time to complete all the track on an average layout, but one has to remember what the track has to achieve, and any faults in it will undoubtedly affect the performance of your trains. There is no escaping this fact at all and so the motto is 'slow and sure'. For those standing at the base of the tree of knowledge, do not be put off by various pundits who claim that track construction is a highly technical job, requiring vast amounts of technical skill, they are only trying to impress you. At the same time, don't underestimate the importance of the subject because the standard of running depends upon the standard of workmanship.

Tools and Materials

Only basic tools are needed as follows:

Soldering iron and solder.
Fine-toothed saw such as X-acto (medium blade).
Two track gauges.
Snips.
Spacing template, (see **Fig 1**).
Quantity of rail; bullhead or flat-bottom.
Quantity of copper-clad (Paxolin-based) sleepers.
Quantity of wooden sleepers, (1.5mm thick ply).

For wooden sleepers, any old off-cuts of ply can be used and this is a useful way of employing those odd scraps. The easiest way is to cut the wood into strips first and then, using one of the copper-clad sleepers, cut them to length with a pen-knife or similar knife so that the wooden sleepers are of identical size to the copper-clad ones.

Construction

First make the template as shown in Fig 1. This can be any length you wish, preferably made from ⅛in ply. The important part is the depth and spacing of the slots. A metal template is not advised because it is more expensive to make and, also the heat from the iron will be dissipated by the metal template, making soldering unstable.

Now to actual construction of the trackwork. Note that the method is only for plain track.

Into each template groove, slot one of the copper-clad sleepers, copper-face uppermost. Taking a length of rail, solder the first sleeper to the rail, ensuring that the rail is close up against the template edge and in an upright position, and at the same time ensuring that the sleeper is hard against the back of the groove. Travelling along the template, solder the rail to all sleepers (**Fig 2**). On reaching the end of the template, draw the assembly along the template and, fitting the last soldered sleeper into the first slot, repeat the process until all the rail has been used up. Remove the assembly from the template and you are left holding a single length of rail with sleepers spaced evenly along its length. To save time you can make as many of these assemblies as are required.

Taking one partially assembled item, place it in position on the layout and with drawing pins, pin each sleeper, (not too hard or you will fracture them), ensuring that they hold the track firmly in position. At this stage form the rail into the shape required, either curved or straight. Now taking a second rail, and using the track gauges spaced about 2in apart, solder the second rail to the sleepers. You will find that the second rail follows the alignment of the first. Watch out for kinks as these may alter the gauge. Having finished this task, the assembly can now be removed, its appearance being like that of standard gauge track on broad-gauge sleepers. Not to worry. It will be noticed that the finished assembly holds its shape. This should be handled carefully and laid on a flat surface out of the way if not for immediate use in the next operation.

Turn the assembly upside-down and taking the wooden sleepers, stick them to the underside of the rails, starting off with the central sleepers. This will help to ensure even spacing between the sleepers generally. Three wooden ones are required to fill each of the spaces between the copper sleepers shown in **Fig 3**.

UHU adhesive is sufficient to hold the wooden sleepers in place under the rails. The wooden ones are mainly for effect, the copper sleepers being the primary means of securing the track to the baseboards.

Turning the track face up again, now paint the sleepers using Rowney PVA raw umber with a tiny dash of PVA cobalt blue for toning effects. Both kinds of sleepers must be painted, having ensured first that the copper surface is cut to prevent shorting out between the rails. Care must be taken to cut only the copper stripping. Do not cut through

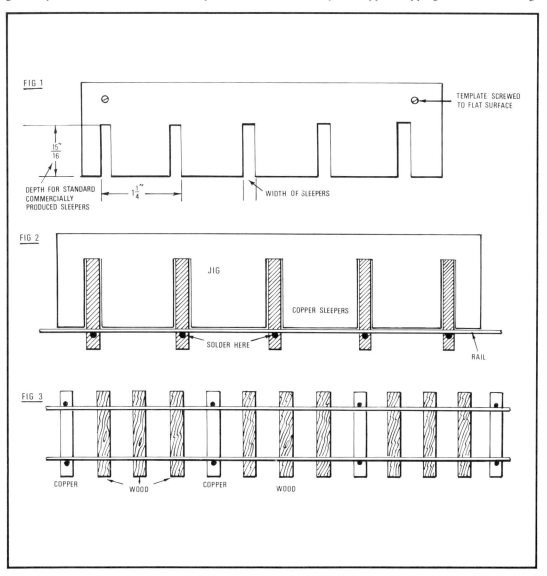

FIG 1

TEMPLATE SCREWED TO FLAT SURFACE

$\frac{15''}{16}$

DEPTH FOR STANDARD COMMERCIALLY PRODUCED SLEEPERS

$1\frac{1}{4}''$

WIDTH OF SLEEPERS

FIG 2

JIG

COPPER SLEEPERS

SOLDER HERE

RAIL

FIG 3

COPPER

WOOD

COPPER

WOOD

the paxolin, the latter material being an insulator anyway. It is best to cut the grooves close to one of the rails (inside web) to reduce any unsightly effects. PVA, if watered down too much, will not take on metals of any kind and so the ratio should be three parts paint to one part water. Rowney PVA can be purchased at any Art Shop.

Having made up the piece of track, painted it, and checked it out for good assembly and workmanship, it can now be fitted to the layout. Ensure that the ends of the rails are squared, with all burrs removed. Coat the area on which the track will rest with a thin coat of Resin W. Lower the track into it and press down hard, at the same time covering the whole area with granite ballast. Add weights to the track ensuring that the ballast does not get under the sleepers, and leave to dry out, after which the surplus ballast is brushed away with a large soft brush. Clean out any paint from the inside webs of the rails and check for ballast which may have stuck to the same areas, as both will affect the running of trains.

It will be noticed that the raw umber goes on a medium brownish colour but dries out to a dark brown reminiscent of the real thing.

There are several ways to join the rails. Fishplates are unreliable and tend to work loose after a time, and so they must be backed up by bonding. This is a process of soldering a thin wire between one piece of track and the next around the joints. Joining by bonding only is unreliable in that in time and with train movement, the track may work out of line causing the ends of the rails to be out of alignment, a common cause of bad running. I favour soldering and bonding, whereby the rail joints are soldered over in a similar fashion to modern continuous welded rail, backed up by bonding wires across joints. There is one snag to this method, which is that by forming continuous rail, no allowance is made for expansion in hot weather. This method must not be used unless, like me, you have a room which is kept at a constant low temperature, the same temperature in which the track was assembled in the first place. It is no good for layouts which are forever changing sites, especially exhibition layouts in which case, use the fishplate and bonding method, thus allowing a means of expansion of the rails and at the same time, providing good continuity through the bonding wire.

Assuming that all locomotives are in top condition, well run in, and that all major electrical apparatus is sound, the only other thing that can cause bad running is the track. The likely faults are as follows:

Misalignment of rail ends between sections. Ensure that all rails are in line, both vertically and horizontally.

Running surfaces of the rails not parallel. (One rail may be too high over its opposite number.) Resolder, the offending rail, and press down hard to ensure parallel surfacing.

Bad joints. All soldered joints must be 'clean, bright and tight'.

Dirty running surfaces to the rails.

Foreign bodies between the webs, especially on the inside of the rails where the wheel flanges pass.

Bad feed return connections on the rails. Also applies to isolators.

Shorting out caused by insufficient cutting off copper sleepers between the rails.

To many, this will sound like old stuff, but it won't do any of us any harm to be reminded of our obligations once in a while.

One point which I forgot to mention earlier is that when laying tracks across the baseboard joints, it is best to lay an unbroken section and cut the rail afterwards to ensure total alignment between boards. The ends of the track close to the board joints should always be fitted with at least two copper sleepers so that the rail is not left to float across the joints without some physical means of support. It is very easy to damage rail ends near baseboard joints so the more support they have the better.

No mention has been made of pointwork because there are a number of good articles about this matter over which I can offer no improvement beyond one cautionary word regarding the continuity of the current. On no account must any reliance be placed upon contact between point blades and the stock rails for the passage of current. It is a useless and unreliable method. Switches, preferably home-made, are best, and these are covered by other articles and publications.

This method of making plain track will also suit 3mm and 2mm scales, the only difference being the sizing of the template. The slots in the template will fit the standard commercially produced paxolin sleepers for 16.5mm gauge only, adjustment being required for 18mm, 18.2mm, and 18.83mm, where in all cases the slots must be progressively deeper as the gauge widens, this along with the fact that sleeper spacing will vary according to how accurate you wish your measurements to be.

Hornby 'A4' to EM Gauge – the Cheaper Way

H. C. Wilson

The Hornby 'A4' is a pretty good model in its own right. There have been a few articles on converting it to EM gauge, but the one problem they all have is that they usually need a new set of wheels – and that puts up the price of the locomotive by a few pounds. When I looked at the wheels of Hornby's *Mallard*, I noticed that they were tyred, and that the face-to-face measurement was just about right. If I could remove the tyres, file off the front of the tyre and the back of the main part of the wheel, then reassemble the wheel, the back-to-back measurement should be right as well. With nothing to lose, I decided to have a go.

As you may have guessed, demolition is the first stage in the conversion. Remove the screws holding the front and rear trucks, the screw holding the keeper plate, and the two screws holding the eccentric cranks to the centre drivers. The chassis can then be dismantled. Do not take the wheels off their axles, though.

The first job on the wheels is to remove the tyres. They are a press fit on the hubs, so finger pressure may be enough. If not, gentle use of a pair of pliers should do the trick. The tyres come off the front of the wheels, (hold the tyres in your fingers and push the hubs out with your thumbs), and only the outer wheels are tyred. The centre ones have to be treated differently. Now file off the backs of the wheel centres until they are flush, but do not remove any metal from the wheel boss (see **Fig 1**). Take the tyres and remove a little from the flange thickness by rubbing it on an oilstone or a piece of fine emery paper. Scrape the inside of the tyre and the outside of the hub to clean them and to give a biting surface for the glue. Stick the tyres to the hubs using epoxy, but do not put the adhesive all round the rim or you will lose your current collectors. Three patches of adhesive will be enough. Make sure that the back of

the tyre is flush with the rear face of the wheel centre. Put it aside to dry. The best way to do this is to cut a couple of slots in a piece of plywood so the wheel backs can rest on it with the axle in the slot. When all four tyres have set, file the fronts of tyres flush with the wheel faces, or nearly so, depending on the tread thickness available. The centre drivers have no tyres, so all you can do is to file the backs, leaving the wheels thinner but flangeless. If you want flanged centre drivers, you may be able to get some outer drivers from Hornby and modify them.

Check the back-to-back measurements, then check that the rims are still electrically connected to the centres. If they are not, drill a small hole between the tyre and the centre, and either push a piece of wire into the hole or fill it with solder.

Reassemble the wheels and valve gear and make sure it runs freely. The front bogie needs new wheels, with spacing washers.

The rear truck needs one or two minor changes. Break off the lug which holds the wheels in, and remove the wheels. Cut off the two strips of metal which take the current to the tender, leaving a 'washer'. Cut off the back part of the drawbar if you want to have a closer coupled tender. File the drawbar to half its thickness, removing the metal from the top to allow the correct size wheels to be used in the trailing truck. File off the remains of the wheel-holding lug. Drill a new hole for the tender coupling hook (there is a small hole which you can enlarge) and make two small holes under the truck to fit a wheel retaining wire (see **Fig 2**). The wheels need pin-point axles and it is easy to point the ends in a hand drill. Drop them in place and use a piece of wire to stop them from falling out.

Remove the tender body, and remove the red lead. Solder the plain end of this lead to the 'washer' on the drawbar.

The mechanism is held in place by two lugs. It can be removed with the aid of a screwdriver used as a lever. Pull the wheels off their axles – you probably won't need a punch. Two jigs are needed now. One is a piece of ⅛in ply, with a hole in it to clear the gears on the wheels; the other is a strip of metal with a 2mm hole in it. Place a geared wheel, gear down, over the hole and press out the plastic centre. Then gently press the tyre on again so that the gear is about 1mm out from the flange (see **Fig 3**). Do the same for the other geared wheels. Place the strip of metal on the jaws of a vice, and use a small punch to push the axle about 1mm into the wheel. You can make new axles if you wish, but I did not find it necessary. Replace the wheels, using washers to reduce side play.

Left:
Ex-LNER 'A4' 4-6-2 No 60027 *Merlin* **at Edinburgh Waverley.** *LPC/IA Library*

Make a hole in the floor of the tender next to where the collector wire was fixed, large enough for the wire to go through with plenty of play. Drill a small hole near the pointed end of the drawbar hook to allow a piece of wire to be inserted and bent to semi-permanently couple the locomotive and tender.

Replace the mechanism in the tender, couple the locomotive to the tender, and put a piece of wire in the hole in the drawbar hook. Next thread the collector wire through the hole in the tender floor and connect it to the motor, then replace the tender body.

Two final comments. The alteration to the collector wire was because I noticed that the original connection tended to lift the trailing truck. Extra detail is well worth adding, but that depends on your own preference, and is beyond the scope of this article.

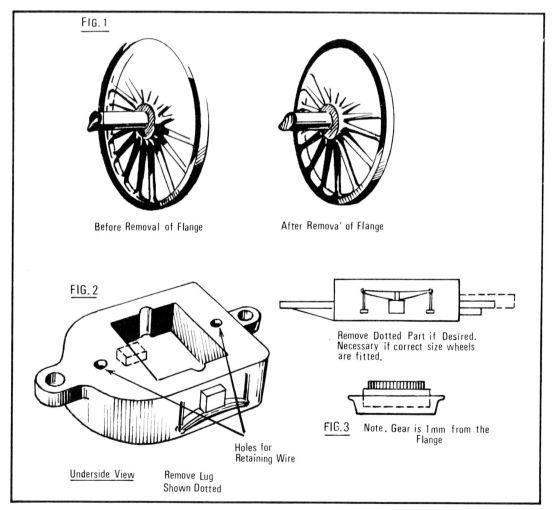

FIG. 1

Before Removal of Flange

After Removal of Flange

FIG. 2

Remove Dotted Part if Desired. Necessary if correct size wheels are fitted.

FIG. 3 Note. Gear is 1mm from the Flange

Holes for Retaining Wire

Underside View

Remove Lug Shown Dotted

My Signals Work Now!

R. M. Stevenson

Like a great number of railway modellers I'm inclined to be lazy and never seem to have enough time to do all the things that I want to or should do. I am always looking for short cuts and the quick way of doing things. After all, it is my layout, and visitors either do not notice or are too polite to mention any of the omissions and inaccuracies.

Take signals for example. How many of you reading this either do not have any at all on your layout, or if you do they don't work? They are there for effect only, to make it all look very railway-like and efficient. Mine was like that too until recently. Oh yes, I knew how to signal the layout but it was too much bother to rig up all the cranks and rodding to make them work. The right ones were put up in the right place and that was it.

So what changed all that? Well, like all these things, the idea just happened and it is reasonably easy to do. So with all the usual disclaimers this is how I went about it.

I used a Ratio signal, a Peco point motor and one of the point motor adaptors made by Kirkton Model Products. By clipping the point motor to the adaptor it becomes a self-contained unit and can be used anywhere. Make up your signal as per the instructions but use a track pin for the angle crank pivot and another one for the bottom of the crank. (see diagram). This latter one projects away from the signal post so that the operating rod from the point motor will move it, so working the signal. Drill a 5/16in hole where your signal is to be placed and screw the adaptor with the motor attached underneath. If, like me, your combined baseboard and track underlay is too thick, the operating rod may not be long enough but extension tubing is available to overcome this. Looking at the signal

from the front, ensure that the motor is switched to the right and place the signal with the projecting track pin resting against the operating rod. Fix the signal down. When the point motor is switched to the left the operating rod will move the crank and the signal arm will drop to 'clear'. The counterweight will now have to be weighted. If you have a friend who is a fisherman ask him for one of his lead pellet weights – they are ideal. When the point motor is switched back again the counterweight will drop the crank so returning the signal to 'danger'.

So there you are, a fairly straightforward job now giving you no excuse not to have working signals and you can also wire up the signal to the point motor so that they work in conjunction.

Go on – try it – you'll be surprised at the difference it makes.

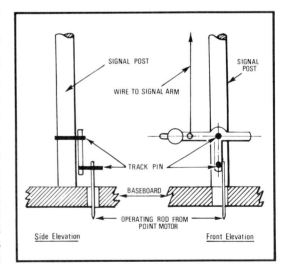

Choosing Scenic Aircraft

Stan Stead

From time to time in the model press someone puts forward the idea of an airport as a scenic addition to a model railway layout. Usually the exercise takes the form of a tiny section of airport, apron or taxiway to fill an awkward corner, since to model even a small aerodrome in its entirety would require a large amount of space even in 2mm scale. Some recent projects involving aircraft models had me visiting local model shops to find aircraft kits, and it seemed that a brief review of the model aircraft kit scene might be useful.

I had been out of touch with plastic model aircraft kits for some years and the job of locating suitable aeroplanes to fit a variety of railway-side scenic applications threw up some interesting problems. In recent years the plastic kit market has contracted quite considerably. It is notable that, while the market for model railway equipment has been fairly static in recent years, the number and variety of proprietary models has continued to grow to the extent that the modeller is spoilt for choice. In the plastic kit field this has generally not been the case. A shrinking market for plastic aircraft has been matched by fewer new models, while the disappearance of older models and the loss of some complete ranges has left the model shop shelves with rather less choice than previously. Of course, overall expansion in other areas such as military models and large scale road vehicles reflects a shifting of interest among the kit builders.

The Question of Scale

Scale is, of course, the most vital consideration in selecting model aircraft to accompany a model railway. As a general rule, few if any aircraft kit ranges are matched to recognised model railway scales. Where perspective modelling can be employed this is not too important. For instance, an aircraft which is undersize can be posed well above or towards the back of the layout to reduce the apparent discrepancy. Similarly, an overscale aircraft may be acceptable if it is right in the foreground, but in such circumstances other models such as road vehicles which are correctly scaled and would give the game away, must be kept away from the aircraft.

Compromise inevitably plays an important role. A popular scale for aircraft models is 1:72 and as this is quite close to the 1:76 of 4mm scale model railways, models in these scales are frequently mixed without any major problems. While this is fine for 4mm scale modellers, whether using OO, EM or P4 track, it is quite another matter for workers in HO gauge. Although their track gauge is the same as OO, the 3.5mm: 1ft scale gives a ratio of 1:87 which makes an aircraft in 1:72 scale appear enormous. The British modeller in 4mm scale is

Below:
A Gatwick-style arrangement is perhaps the ultimate model railway/airport link-up, but it does not have to represent current practice. Already a piece of history is this view of a British Airways Viscount passing over a Class 423 unit on a Gatwick service. *BR*

thus in luck, while his counterpart modelling European or North American railways will have problems finding aircraft scaled to suit his needs.

The N gauge modeller's luck will depend on his particular requirements. If he is seeking small aircraft types, military and light planes, he may have problems. However, the N gauge modeller seeking larger airliners (and he may well have room for a section of Gatwick-style airport close to his line) will be able to get away with the 1:144 series in the Airfix range. This is quite close to the 1:148 of British N gauge.

Let us now look at some specific instances.

Military Aircraft

A corner of a military airfield can make an interesting and attractive scenic addition to the layout. Large amounts of space are not necessary and in most instances all that's needed for an older style location would be a Nissen hut or two, some appropriate fencing to keep out the curious and

Below:
This section of airport diorama was featured in *MRC* nearly 20 years ago and took Gatwick as its inspiration. The EMU was a conversion by Albert Goodall and the structures were a mixture of kits and scratchbuilt items. Aircraft were all commercially available but in hand-painted liveries. The Lufthansa Boeing 737 was a 1:72 Aurora kit. This and the Dinky Piper in the foreground are now obsolete, but the Dakota is still available in liveries other than BUA. The Boeing 727 on finals was an Airfix 1:144 kit hand-painted in Wardair livery and demonstrates the use of a smaller-than-scale aircraft to give perspective.

Right:
The GWR 150 celebrations of summer 1985 looked set to give some prominence to the Great Western's pioneering of internal air services through the repainting of a preserved Dragon Rapide in Railway Air Services livery. The RAS timetable of 1939 shows the logo and the red and green colour scheme.

sufficient tarmac standing area for an aircraft or two. For the early, between-the-wars period one could get away with a grass field and smaller, older aircraft.

By far the widest choice of prototype is available in military aircraft to 1:72 scale. My researches were carried out in typical toy and model shops, so most of the types I found are commonplace and easy to obtain. It is important to match the aircraft to the period of the layout, just as one should with road vehicles. With the wide variety available in this category, this is no great problem. In small fighter aircraft the modeller can select from biplanes of the Great War period, the Sopwith Camel and Bristol Fighter, for instance, through 1930s types such as the Hawker Fury, Gloster Gladiator and Fairey Swordfish. Then there are World War 2 types in profusion, Spitfires and Hurricanes of course, but also larger aircraft such as the Mosquito and even the Lancaster. Bombers of the latter size are pretty large beasts in 1:72 and are likely to be of less interest unless there is a large area of layout to fill.

Prominent in the High Street stores are the ranges of Airfix and Matchbox which include most of the types mentioned plus a host of other complementary types. The Airfix range has shrunk somewhat and in many instances the Matchbox kits tend to dominate. They are every bit as good as the Airfix and are

sometimes moulded in several colours to reduce the need for painting. Other ranges also include kits in 1:72 scale, for instance Heller and Revell. These are respectively French and American made, and accordingly the number of British outline models they produce is rather limited. There are other makes too, particularly Italian and Japanese imports, but again most of their prototypes will not be of interest on a British layout. In some instances, particularly concerning American kits, beware if a scale is not quoted on the box, since some makes such as Monogram do not maintain a constant scale.

Modern military aircraft are also well covered in all these ranges, but such types are not particularly relevant to our needs since they would tend to be shut away in hangars and not posed alongside a railway for everyone to see!

For layouts based in the 'Big Four' (1923-48) period a simple set-piece scene can be created with a suitable aircraft backed up by ground support vehicles from the Airfix range. There are the Emergency set and Rescue set, each with two road vehicles, and there was also a 'Queen Mary' aircraft transporter, although I have not seen this in the shops lately.

Prewar Civil Aircraft

Consideration of this aspect was prompted by the news that the GWR 150 celebrations in 1985 were to include a Dragon Rapide aircraft painted in Railway Air Services colours to mark the Great Western's involvement in early internal passenger air services. The Great Western inaugurated

Below:
A glimpse inside the RAS timetable. A warning to passengers to arrive at least 10 minutes before departure time makes an interesting comparison with today's airport arrangements!

internal air services with a Cardiff-Bristol-Birmingham route flown by Westland Wessex aircraft. Within a year Railway Air Services had been formed to take over the internal air service interests of the GWR and the Southern Railway, and a network of routes including the Isle of Wight and Channel Islands was established.

Among the types flown by RAS were the three-engined Wessex, twin-engined de Havilland Dragon bi-plane and the four-engined DH-86, I could find none of these in model form and so settled for a delightful kit of the DH-89 Dragon Rapide in 1:72 scale by Heller. This is similar to a small version of the DH-86 and I was halfway through painting the model to match an illustration of one of these, when I found that RAS owned at least two Dragon Rapides, registrations G-ACPP *City of Bristol* and G-ACPR *City of Birmingham.*

Some 685 Dragon Rapides were built and the Heller kit includes decals for three typical examples. Finishing in RAS livery meant hand-painting the model, however, for which a No 00 paint brush and a steady hand are required. I decided to line the fuselage before assembly, using a bow pen and thinned paint. The RAS colours were red and green with white lettering on the company name and emblem. Incidentally, notice how closely the RAS emblem resembles the then-current GWR 'shirt-button' monogram.

The most difficult job in assembling the Heller model is the 'rigging' with fine black thread, but it is well worth the effort as it really gives the model character. Here is a model which is absolutely appropriate to a railway setting, with a fictitious

Below:
The Heller DH89 Dragon Rapide finished as Railway Air Services G-ACPP *City of Bristol*.

airfield close by the main line. Minimal airport facilities are required and the model measures only 8in wingspan, so very little space is needed.

Apart from the Dragon Rapide there are few prewar civil aircraft, due largely to the fact that civil flying was still somewhat in its infancy. Curiously, though irrelevant to railway modelling, none of the kit manufacturers seems to have taken any interest in the assorted flying boats which were the mainstay of long distance operations at the time.

Postwar Civil Aircraft

Following World War 2, both ex-military aircraft and pilots were available for civil flying and many early post-war airliners and freighters were either adapted military aircraft or designs which used major components which had proved successful in wartime service.

From the modelling viewpoint the Dakota is of obvious interest. Many thousands were built during the war as the C-47 transport and subsequently as the DC-3 or Dakota for civil use. At first used for freighting and as front-line short-haul airliners, Dakotas remain in use throughout the world in a variety of roles, although the handful of UK survivors in regular use are freighters. For a short time after the war, Railway Air Services had three

Below:
Westland Wessex G-ACZP of Railway Air Services. No suitable model kit of this aircraft is available, but modellers wishing to create a 1930s airport could do no better than to base their buildings on the control tower visible in this view. *Real Photographs*

Bottom:
The DH86 was the so-called 'express' aircraft of Railway Air Services, a four-engined enlarged Dragon Rapide. G-ACVY *Mercury* **shows a painting style similar to that of the Dragon Rapide.** *Real Photographs*

aircraft of the type, one at least (G-AGZB) carrying RAS livery until absorption into the newly formed British European Airways.

The Airfix 1:72 scale Dakota was an excellent model, produced in a variety of guises. The civil version is no longer available, but a C-47 Gunship version is still produced and requires little conversion. Various other C-47 kits are available, requiring little more than an appropriate paint job to fit them for civil use, and remember they could even be relevant on a modern image layout. Esci produce theirs as a DC-3 in TWA livery and as a military C-47.

Airfix also produced a number of other useful post-war civil aircraft, but again one is likely to be scouring the swap-meets for unbuilt examples and probably paying a high price too. Among the most memorable are the D.H. Heron, a diminutive four-engine job which required a hefty ballast weight in the nose to keep it standing on its tricycle undercarriage, a useful Bristol Super Freighter with opening nose doors and complete with car loading ramps, and an Aer Lingus Fokker Friendship.

Alas, these are gone, and the early post-war scene is somewhat thin in civil aircraft. For long-range use, but small by modern standards, there is a Lockheed Constellation in 1:72 by Heller. This American airliner was widely used by airlines flying into the UK as well as by British Overseas Airways (BOAC) during the early 1950s, and is supplied with decals for Air France and TWA. Also in this series is a Douglas DC6B and a Boeing 707 is promised for 1985 production.

Current airliners, being generally rather large, are not particularly suited to modelling in 1:72 scale. The field is, however, well covered in 1:144 which is passable for N gauge. Revell has a Superconstellation in this scale. The prototype first flew in 1950 and is an ideal post-war civil airliner model, but this apart, N gauge modellers will not find much in that period to help them. Where they do score well is in modern airliners, where Revell offers a Boeing 747 'Jumbo' in KLM or Lufthansa livery, a 727 and a 707 both in Lufthansa colours. For the same German airline they also offer the Douglas DC10-30. N scale modellers also have the remnants of the Airfix 1:144 scale range which are still available in some stores. Included in this range are the BAC One-Eleven and Concorde.

Heller's civil aircraft range also features current types, but in 1:125 scale. These might be passable for 3mm scale users, particularly the Caravelle which is the only one reproduced to 1:100 scale. In the 1:125 range Heller features the Lockheed Tristar, Boeing 727, 737 and 747, Douglas DC9 and DC10, Concorde, and the A300 Airbus. All are supplied in colour schemes in which they could regularly be seen in the UK. Revell has a Douglas DC-9 in 1:120 decorated for KLM (Royal Dutch Airlines).

Floatplanes

This is another area which can be quite quickly summed up. In terms of civil types likely to be of interest for railway modellers the field is limited and restricted almost entirely to 1:72 types. One notable exception is the Esci Cessna 172 seaplane in 1:48 which could be used with gauge 0.

In the 1:72 field the only readily available civil floatplane of a small nature is the Matchbox Noorduyn Norseman, a 1939 Canadian design which looks sufficiently modern to pass muster on a post-war layout, indeed some are still in service. The kit is moulded in three colours and comes with markings for civil or military use, as well as a choice of wheeled undercarriage, floats or skis.

The Canadair CL-215 is well-known as the flying boat 'water-bomber' widely used in fighting forest

Above:

Interesting ground support vehicles like these surrounding a British Airways Boeing 707 at Heathrow could be adapted from proprietary die cast models.

fires in Canada, France and Spain. Heller's 1:72 kit is attractive but not really typical for British modellers. Here, the Airfix Sunderland might stand conversion for civil use. Also in 1:72 Revell has the PBY 6A Catalina as used by Jacques Cousteau. This American flying boat of World War 2 vintage was quite widely converted for civilian uses.

While this was in preparation, Matchbox introduced their excellent DHC Twin Otter, a 20-seat passenger aircraft which is widely used in Europe and North America. The model is thus well suited to a British layout based on modern (post-1970s) practice. The Matchbox kit comes with choice of wheels, floats or skis but, of the transfers for Canadian Armed Forces or Aurigny (Channel Isles) Airlines, only the latter will be useful.

Modern Light aircraft

These are, perhaps, the most suitable aircraft models for a layout based on current railway practice and yet here the 4mm scale modeller must leave the field to workers in the larger scales. I could find nothing readily available in 1:72 scale although I am tolerably certain that I have seen some 'private jets' of HS 125 and Learjet type in recent years in this scale.

Modellers in gauge 0 would get away with the Esci Cessna 172 Skyhawk in 1:48 – the typical modern light plane. In 1:50, Heller has the Cessna 150 Commuter and Skymaster 2, as well as several compatible European types and some helicopters. Revell does even better with a Beech Bonanza V35, Cessna 150, Piper Cherokee and Super Cub, Mooney Super 21 and Aero Subaru, all in 1:48 scale.

For other more specific requirements, one can only look outside the readily available plastic kits, at such areas as vacuum-formed and limited run models which are generally available only through specialist aviation modelling sources.

Above:
The Matchbox Noorduyn Norseman is an attractive model which can be built with wheels, floats or skis. It is to 1:72 scale.

Below:
Heller's Canadair CL-215 'Water-bomber' finished in a fictitious livery as a forest fire fighter. The kit comes with French markings.

Above:
The DH Twin Otter is a popular and widely used 20-seater. This float-equipped example belonging to Air BC was seen at Victoria, British Columbia, in 1981.

Below:
The Twin Otter is a recent release in the Matchbox 1:72 range, supplied with wheels, floats or skis and with markings for Canadian Armed Forces or Aurigny (Channel Islands). This example was hand-painted in Air BC livery.